Lone Wolf

HOW EMIRATES TEAM NEW ZEALAND
STUNNED THE WORLD

RICHARD GLADWELL

mower

Contents

Preface

My first encounter with the America's Cup happened in a draughty school hall at Westlake Boys in November 1967 during a School Certificate English exam. One of the questions was to write about a significant sporting event.

Suddenly I had this flash of inspiration: I'd write about the 1962 America's Cup between *Weatherly* and *Gretel* when the Australian Challenger surfed past the Defender to give the crew from Down Under their first race win.

Since late 1983 I have covered the America's Cup for various publications, and since mid-2005 for Sail-World.com, the world's largest online sailing news network.

The shift to online media has meant that the days are gone of getting a scoop and carefully guarding it for a couple of weeks while your magazine goes through the print and distribution process. Now it is instant.

The next America's Cup competitive cycle starts as soon as the current match is over.

Part of that cycle is getting the money together as soon as you can. Hiring the best design, sailing and engineering teams you can afford, and getting sponsors and investors on board. They are all harbingers of the outcome of the next match.

The Cup is a game of chess. One team makes a move. The other either responds to counter, moves in a different direction or does nothing. Spotting those moves and putting them into context for Cup fans is the role of the sailing media, knowing that a team will tell you exactly what they want you to hear.

The America's Cup is a time-management exercise — a test of who can develop the fastest boat within the prescribed time in the Cup cycle. All of the teams in the 2017 America's Cup ran out of time. The team that won stuck to a simple and effective campaign strategy and made the best use of the available time and resources.

This is the story of that team and the 35th America's Cup.

Richard Gladwell
August 2017

Introduction

At 2.33 pm on the afternoon of 26 June 2017, Emirates Team New Zealand crossed the finish line in Bermuda's Great Sound to win the premier trophy in sailing. The 8–1 win in Bermuda was the third for the most successful professional sailing team in history.

New Zealand's America's Cup legacy was born in late March 1984, when Marcel Fachler, a Sydney-based, Belgian-born businessman, lodged a challenge with the Royal Perth Yacht Club on behalf of a New Zealand club — the Royal New Zealand Yacht Squadron.

The Squadron was unaware of Fachler's move, but took up his offer of funding a feasibility study and establishing an organis-ational framework for a challenge for the then 133-year-old trophy.

That started a 30-year involvement by New Zealand, which has spanned three iterations.

The first was New Zealand Challenge, headed by Sir Michael Fay from 1987 to 1992, which also covered the 'Big Boat' challenge of 1988. New Zealand fell in love with the America's Cup in Fremantle and all its drama.

That love affair continued with the 1995–2000 Team New Zealand led by Sir Peter Blake and Alan Sefton, who twice won yachting's premier trophy. Emirates Team New Zealand is the current team and since March 2003 has been led by Grant Dalton and Kevin Shoebridge, winning for the third time in June 2017.

Although New Zealand is the smallest country to have contested the America's Cup, the Kiwis have been the most innovative. First with the fibreglass yacht in 1987, then the 120-ft Big Boat in 1988, and the tandem keel in 1992.

NZL-32, the winner in 1995, was simply a very well-designed yacht which took her synergy from a lot of small design and engineering nuances, along with an outstanding crew and a superbly led team, to produce New Zealand's first win.

The same formula was repeated for the second win in 2000. Key design innovations included the 'Ice Breaker' bow to get more speed from a longer effective sailing length plus the Millennium rig from Southern Spars together with a top sailing crew and a well-led team.

New Zealand brought foiling to the 2013 America's Cup and changed the sport. The 2017 match saw a repeat of the 1995 and 2000 formula — design and engineering innovation, a top sailing crew and a well-led team.

The America's Cup does have its dark side. Learning to cope, innovate and succeed in the face of adversity is another of the vital lessons of success — and was no more so for the team that won the Cup in Bermuda on 26 June 2017.

Chapter 1

Poised on a knife edge

Day 2 of the Challenger Final was reckoned to be the turning point of the 35th America's Cup for Emirates Team New Zealand.

The Kiwis came away with two wins from three races, despite being caught out with their light-weather daggerboards in a breeze that rose and fell during the afternoon.

After their America's Cup win, Emirates Team New Zealand skipper Glenn Ashby picked that crucial day as being a major confidence booster for the campaign, its direction and capability.

'My thinking was that if we could race well against Artemis in breezy conditions — given that they had beaten Oracle in 17 races in a row — then we possibly might have a chance at the Cup,' he said.

As the only crew member with previous America's Cup experience aboard the New Zealand Challenger, Ashby says he knew they were going to have a big battle with Artemis Racing in the Challenger Final.

'If we could outsail them in these conditions, we could keep on our path and keep improving ourselves and the boat,' said the 2008 Olympic Silver medallist and multiple world champion in several multihull classes.

It was a dramatic day on the Great Sound in Bermuda, which is formed from the sunken inner crater of a 30 million-year-old volcano, located 640 nautical miles off the US coast in the Atlantic Ocean.

Three races were scheduled.

After being treated to almost a month of fine weather, the skies opened over Bermuda as a front passed over the Atlantic Ocean archipelago dropping much-needed rain. The downpour was preceded by a spectacular thunderstorm overnight with lightning and it was still raining as the boats left the team bases located in the historic Royal Naval Dockyard, a few hundred metres from the race course.

Emirates Team New Zealand heads for the finish in the Challenger Final, Race 6, which they won by 1 second. — RICHARD GLADWELL

Team meteorologists, critical to making the correct call on foil selection, were perplexed with the change in weather system, with a front set to pass over Bermuda.

On the morning of the second day of racing with the New Zealand team poised on a 2–1 lead in the best of nine series, rain was falling, and winds had been up to 25 kts in strength — beyond the upper limit for racing.

'Everything is on the table,' Race Director Iain Murray told the mid-morning media briefing. 'When the team forecasters are ringing us and saying "What do you know?" I think that is indicative of the situation out there.'

Murray put up an overhead showing two weather sources predicting winds from the south-west, and explained that forecast was the thinking of the teams. However, as he spoke the wind was blowing at 20 kts from the opposite direction — north-east.

Nearer to race start time, the breeze dropped in strength to 6 kts gusting 10 kts. The right strength but opposite direction of the forecasts. Predictwind.com, the weather forecasting application developed by Jon Bilger, a forecaster for Alinghi, twice winner of the America's Cup, put the wind strength at 10–14 kts at race start time. Even the independent forecasters couldn't agree.

The sudden-death Challenger Final was poised on a knife edge.

Emirates Team New Zealand had emerged from the first day's racing with a lucky come-from-behind, 2–1 scorecard — after Artemis Racing's helmsman Nathan Outteridge slipped on a crossbeam, after getting caught by an unexpected change in G-force, and went overboard during a critical tack. The Swedish Challenger withdrew from the race. 'Not the first time it has happened,' he quipped later. Emirates Team New Zealand was ahead before the mishap.

With a 2–1 points score and a possible three

Emirates Team New Zealand and Artemis Racing at top speed on Leg 1, Race 4 of the Challenger Final. — RICHARD GLADWELL

wins from the three races scheduled on Day 2 of the Challenger Final, the Kiwis were within striking distance of collecting the required 5 points and becoming the Challenger for their third successive America's Cup Match.

The confused weather data meant that correct foil selection was even more critical to the performance of the 50-ft wingsailed catamarans, which fly above the water on hydrofoils at up to four times the actual windspeed.

Generally speaking, two sets of daggerboards (as the foils in the centre of the AC50 are known) are allowed. Most teams opt for a light-weather set to provide more lift more quickly, and a second all-purpose set for medium to heavy air winds. The all-purpose daggerboards are narrower and, because of the reduced size, offer less drag through the water, and are therefore faster. The light-air daggerboards are bigger, lift the 2400-kg catamarans out of the water more quickly and are faster in lighter weather.

Making the wrong daggerboard selection for the conditions can put one boat at a significant disadvantage — if their opponent has made the correct choice. But, of course, if both teams have their weather forecast and foil choice wrong, then it becomes a question of how far the incorrect daggerboard choice can effectively operate beyond its designed range of wind.

Earlier in the regatta there had been at least a couple of instances when highly fancied teams had scored an upset loss against a bottom-of-the-table team, attributed to the wrong choice of foils.

To complicate matters even further the foil-selection call had ideally to be made the night before to allow shore crews time to prepare the race boat. Official measurement checks were scheduled for nine o'clock on the morning of the race, and the foil selections were locked in for the day. Given those processes and schedule, it is not possible to rectify an incorrect foil selection between races — the teams were stuck with their decision for the duration of the day's racing.

At this stage of the Challenger Selection Series, or Playoffs as organisers had named them for this America's Cup, the fate of the teams in their four-year, $90 million America's Cup programmes hung on the accuracy of a single weather forecast.

Tension mounted as the two teams realised that they had each made a different call on foil selection. Emirates Team New Zealand had opted for a choice of lighter air foils while Artemis Racing had opted for their all-purpose set. One would be right and the other wrong — with the latter's America's Cup campaign hanging in the balance.

The game looked to be up for Emirates Team New Zealand as winds puffed to 15 kts at the start of Race 4, well past the expected range for their light-air boards. The body language was palpable aboard the Kiwi chase boat as the coaches and analysts realised they had fitted the wrong boards and could be on the losing end of a 4–2 scoreline in a couple of hours.

'Our forecast was different from Team New Zealand — going out there it was gusting 15 to 16 knots — and we were quite happy with our configuration,' said Nathan Outteridge after the racing. 'But on a day like today, the weather can be quite unstable and change quickly.'

The first race of the day and Race 4 of the Challenger Final got away to an even start. Artemis Racing, helmed by Nathan Outteridge, an Olympic Gold and Silver medallist in the Olympic

49er skiff class, led from start to finish, winning by a 15-second margin, with the boats hitting 40 kts on the final leg to the finish.

That was despite a near disaster for the Swedes as they crashed off their foils at the end of the final beat to windward and briefly lost control, with the Kiwis having to take avoiding action and unsuccessfully protesting.

The result evened the Finals score at two races apiece.

The pendulum swung the Kiwis' way in the second race of the day, or Race 5 in the Final Series, as the breeze dropped to 11 kts at the race start time.

Outteridge beat his old adversary in the 49er, Peter Burling, over the start line and led around Mark 1, with the America's Cup Class (ACC) yachts hitting 43 kts — in just 11 kts of breeze and flat water. That's almost four times the speed of the wind.

As the breeze lightened, Emirates Team New Zealand found conditions to their liking and more within the range of their foil selection. They passed the Swedish team on the second leg and had an easy win after Sweden withdrew for the second time in the five races sailed so far in the Final Series.

Both boats suffered issues with their onboard hydraulic and electrical systems. Emirates Team New Zealand had support crew aboard between the first two races working in the wingsail trimmer's cockpit. Artemis Racing gave up in Race 5, preferring to resolve their electrical issues caused by a faulty switch, and made the decision to fix the issue and be ready for the final race of the day.

Outteridge put the switch issue down to the heavy rain getting into the electrics and causing one of the buttons to misfire and latch in the on position. 'It occurred in the first race and we couldn't fault-find before the second race. When it presented itself again in the second race, we then had a better idea of where it was coming from. So instead of sailing out the course we decided to use the time to fix the problem, so we were ready for the third race.'

The breeze stayed around 11–12 kts for the start of Race 6, with another even start. Artemis once again had the lead after the high-

TOP: Both Artemis Racing and Emirates Team New Zealand worked on systems issues after Race 4 of the Challenger Final. — RICHARD GLADWELL
BOTTOM: Artemis Racing has a nosedive on a downwind leg of Race 5 of the Challenger Final. — RICHARD GLADWELL

speed reach to the first mark. Outteridge led for the first three legs, with Burling snatching a narrow lead after a downwind leg to round Mark 4, just 1 second ahead, or half a boat length.

New Zealand extended to a 15-second lead sailing into the wind on Leg 5 and looked set to move on to Match Point.

Going into Mark 6, the penultimate turning point of the six-leg course, the young Kiwi helmsman made a serious misjudgement of the approach angle to the mark as the catamarans hit 35 kts in just 12 kts of wind.

'It was my mistake, I misjudged the layline for the other gate,' Burling explained after the race.

'The racing is so close that if you make one mistake, a good lead can turn to nothing. Some of the guys in the chase boats say it took a couple of years off their lives,' he joked.

Emirates Team New Zealand almost hit the mark and then gybed without sufficient hydraulic pressure, bringing the red and black catamaran to a near stop, while the Swedish yacht was on a fast approach to windward and headed for the finish.

The New Zealanders' secret weapon, their four 'cyclors' using pedal power to generate the hydraulic pressure necessary to sail the AC50, came into their own, and quickly generated sufficient power to get *Aotearoa* moving again. It was a bow-to-bow drag race for the short leg to the finish line.

Incredibly, Emirates Team New Zealand held on to win by a 1-second margin as both boats swung their bows across the finish line in front of the 10,000 fans in the stadium, who rose to their feet cheering, as the Kiwi crew moved to 4–2 in the series.

Outteridge summed the day up this way: 'We were going really nicely in the first race, and we were able to hold on to the lead and win.

Emirates Team New Zealand rounds the leeward mark in Race 5 of the Challenger Final.

— RICHARD GLADWELL

In the second race, again we got another good start, but the wind went a bit lighter. Team New Zealand had better pace than us upwind, and we had to go into an aggressive tactics mode.

'In the third race, we were more evenly matched.'

'We did have the wrong boards on,' said Emirates Team New Zealand coach Murray Jones after the race. 'That gave us some limitations. Pete and the boys did a fantastic job of doing what they had to do, with what they had on. We were very happy to get out of the day with two wins out of three races,' the now six-times America's Cup winner added.

For the first time in the regatta, Emirates Team New Zealand seemed to have a game plan and stuck to it. As Peter Burling explained at the post-race media conference, the team was not too bothered about the start, but their focus was on being in contact with their opponent at Mark 2.

'Our main goal is to get to the bottom mark in good shape and then chip away from there,' Burling said. Without saying too much, Burling disclosed that the team had a very good 'high mode' where they could, if they wished, both sail closer to the wind than their competitor and at a faster speed. 'We just work into a high groove.'

It had also become apparent that while the brain might be willing, the arm-grinders on the other boats were not physically able to match a sustained close-tacking duel competing against the leg power of the Kiwi cyclors.

The best strategy to beat the Kiwis seemed to be to get in front and hope to stay there — applying the match-racing adage of it being one matter to catch up, but another to pass. Occasionally, this strategy would win a race,

but it became increasingly difficult as the Kiwis could just tack away with minimal speed loss, and then keep throwing in foiling tacks until the cover was broken.

So far, twice in the Challenger Final, the royal blue-hulled Artemis Racing had let Emirates Team New Zealand off the hook. And, given slightly different circumstances, at the end of the second day's racing it could well have been the Kiwis on two wins and Artemis on four. But there is luck in sailing, and Peter Burling is a lucky sailor. Artemis, on the other hand, had a string of 'if only' situations where the game had just not gone their way — including an almost unprecedented situation when an umpire call in the Qualifiers was reversed two hours after being made.

Emirates Team New Zealand went into Day 3 having to win just one of three races.

Lighter winds were forecast for the day, with the windspeed being in single digits for the second time in a month at just 8 kts for the start. These were conditions for which the New Zealanders had optimised their Challenger, after analysing 50 years of Bermudian weather records. They were the conditions in which they had spent two months training alone in Auckland, while their competitors had enjoyed late-scheduled practice racing in Bermuda — organised after it was too late for Emirates Team New Zealand to change their travel and shipping plans.

For the Kiwis, Day 3 of the Challenger Final was their check-in time with reality.

They had come to Bermuda with the expectation of being fast in the light and being able to execute foiling tacks and gybes better than their already resident competitors. Plus, they expected to be able to foil earlier, and sail better angles than the other five teams. Day 3 was their first real test in the conditions expected for the Match in six days' time.

Regatta Director Iain Murray had one attempt at getting a race under way on the Great Sound on the scheduled start time of 2.12 pm and in a breeze that had been piping up to 15 kts before the start.

For a time, it looked as if the Kiwis would be in difficulty again, having once more opted for their gull-wing shaped light-weather boards.

The race had its dramas, and Artemis Racing was a lot closer, even better than the New Zealanders. But racing was abandoned after the wind died completely on Leg 4. Those ashore and afloat were able to witness the weird phenomenon of the AC50s, capable of sailing at four times the windspeed, being unable to sail efficiently to reach the downwind mark because of light winds and some difficult-to-explain apparent wind physics.

After a wait of 90 minutes, Race 7 got under way again in 8 kts of wind, and right on the start time limit — dictated by the required finish time of 5 pm.

Emirates Team New Zealand won the start, again, and led at Mark 1. This time there was no catching the Kiwis, and their margin steadily increased up and down wind with the winning margin being recorded at 56 seconds. That result gave Emirates Team New Zealand their fifth win in the best of nine series and they went forward to be the Challenger for the 35th America's Cup, for the third time in the last three multi-challenger Matches for the America's Cup.

The scene was set for the New Zealanders to have a chance of redemption after their 2013 drubbing in San Francisco at the hands of Oracle Team USA.

Emirates Team New Zealand and Artemis Racing head at top speed for the start line in Race 5 of the Challenger Final. — RICHARD GLADWELL

Chapter 2

The road to redemption

Saturday, 15 February 2003 should have been a great day for Team New Zealand.

They were on their home stadium, under clear skies, and a fresh south-westerly for their second defence of the America's Cup. The team which was in its second rendition (originally New Zealand Challenge from 1987–1992) had not lost a race in the last two Matches in 1995 in San Diego and Auckland in 2000.

The large spectator fleet took up its position around the perimeter of the America's Cup course in the inner Hauraki Gulf, in expectation of the showdown between the Heroes and Villains.

Almost three years after a shock exit from Team New Zealand, Sir Russell Coutts, Olympic Gold medallist at the age of 23 and a double America's Cup-winning skipper, was now sailing for Swiss Challenger Alinghi. He was up against his protégé Dean Barker, and what was left of the Team New Zealand crew of 2000 after billionaire backers had enticed 35 Kiwi sailing crew to join five of the nine challenger teams.

While the New Zealand public had taken Luna Rossa, the 2000 Challenger, to their hearts, they didn't embrace Russell Coutts and five other former Team New Zealand members crewing Alinghi quite so warmly in 2003.

As Nelson signalled ahead of the Battle of Trafalgar, the loyal Team New Zealand fans expected 'every man to do his duty'. However, unbeknown to fans and media, Emirates Team New Zealand had a major structural failure with their trial-horse, *NZL-81*, in December 2012 and her hull and deck failed again just before the start of the 31st America's Cup Match. She was towed to the course each day to keep up appearances, but could never be sailed as a tune-up boat or trial-horse for *NZL-82*.

A few minutes into the race, it was plain that the Defender's boat wasn't up to the task, taking on water as the cockpit flooded in the

Emirates Team New Zealand has three ripped spinnakers set as she loses her lead in Race 5 of the 2007 America's Cup. — CARLO BORLENGHI

fresh 20-kt breeze, the boom broke, and the jib tack ripped out of its bow fitting.

For the first time in 83 years, a Defender withdrew from an America's Cup race. Instead of being remembered as the opening stanza of a successful defence, 15 February 2003 was remembered for the sight of a crew member bailing frantically with a blue bucket.

After a brave fightback in the next two races, the Kiwis capitulated completely after an aluminium spreader tip gave way in a fresh onshore breeze as *NZL-82* ploughed into the steep swell. The 32-metre mast crumpled along with any faint hope of a successful defence.

Two withdrawals and three race losses were not an outcome New Zealand expected of its America's Cup team. Sir Peter Blake's proud legacy of back-to-back wins in 1995 and 2000 was in tatters.

It was an awful series to watch from the media boat. Every day we would get the 'inside' word that these were the conditions in which

NZL-82 would revel, instead, aside from the odd good leg, it got worse as the series progressed.

Grant Dalton, with seven round-the-world races in his logbook, watched the debacle unfold on television. Later that month the Round the World racer was engaged by the Board of Team New Zealand to regenerate the fortunes of the America's Cup team.

'Dalts' had an interesting history with high-profile Kiwi teams. Never being backward about coming forward, he had tried for selection in Peter Blake's *Ceramco New Zealand* crew in the 1981–82 Whitbread Round the World Race, the world's premier ocean race, now the Volvo Ocean Race. He didn't make the cut.

Dalton joined the crew of the Dutch ketch *Flyer II* for the 1981–82 race, together with Erle Williams and Joey Allen, beating Blake and

Crew bail with the now infamous blue bucket on Team New Zealand in Race 1 of the 2003 America's Cup. — IVOR WILKINS

winning the four-leg race around the world.

For the 1985–86 Whitbread, Blake took the brash Dalton into his *Lion New Zealand* crew as a watch captain. But halfway around the world, Dalton announced, to Blake's chagrin, that he would be doing his own boat for the next Whitbread, thank you. That set up one of the greatest sailing contests ever as Dalton, skippering *Fisher & Paykel New Zealand*, fought valiantly against Blake in *Steinlager 2* in the next race.

'Big Red', as *Steinlager 2* became affectionately known, won all six legs of the 1989–90 Round the World Race, a feat that has never been matched. *Fisher & Paykel New Zealand* clocked up big leads on several legs, only for them to end in frustration as the wily Blake slipped through within 24 hours of the finish line.

Grant Dalton skippered the 120-ft catamaran *Club Med* to a win in his seventh race around the world.

Between the Lion New Zealand and Fisher & Paykel campaigns, Dalton tried out for New Zealand's first 1986–87 America's Cup campaign in Fremantle. Although he had a huge ticker and was fanatical about strength and fitness (he'd been a New Zealand power-lifting record holder for his weight), his physical stature didn't slot in easily to the 12 Metre world. Dalton served out the campaign in the trial-horse, as part of the 'mushroom crew' who also wintered over in Fremantle. They did the hard yards but got none of the glory.

Dalton won the next iteration of the Whitbread, skippering the maxi ketch *New Zealand Endeavour*. She was backed by a multitude of New Zealand companies, rather than a single naming rights sponsor. He sailed two Volvo Ocean Races skippering *Merit Cup* to second overall in the 1997–98 edition and *Amer Sport One* in 2001–02, finishing third.

His final win came in a 2001 round-the-world race, open to all comers, and simply

named 'The Race'. Dalton skippered the 120-ft catamaran *Club Med* to win, setting two records in the process — a new 24 hours distance sailed and fastest circumnavigation — despite the giant multihull struggling to hold together structurally in the latter stages of The Race.

For various reasons, Dalton is never really given credit for his significant trans-oceanic racing successes. He also has a record, at least equal to that of Sir Peter Blake, for his ability to raise sponsorship for his sailing projects. In many respects the two are polar opposites. An accountant by training, Dalton is a calculated risk taker and a hard driver on and off the water.

Like Blake, Dalton is an outstanding seaman. He is also a martinet on boat strength and structural integrity. Watching the 2003 demolition of *NZL-82* on television would have been an infuriating experience. To Dalts' credit, he willingly took a hospital pass when Team

Mission accomplished for Team Principal Matteo de Nora (third from right) after 14 years of America's Cup campaigns. — Scott Stallard

New Zealand's managing director's role was offered.

Contrary to expectations, there was not a massacre among the ranks of what was left of Team New Zealand when Dalton walked through the doors of the Halsey Street, Auckland base. As expected, after a formal investigation and publicly released report into the 2003 defence campaign, a few on the design side departed, either of their own volition or given an assisted exit.

Despite his impetuous, shoot-from-the-hip reputation, Dalton went carefully through the team. As a fundraiser, he recognised that a superb $90 million fundraising effort had been undertaken by Tony Thomas. He stayed, as did skipper Dean Barker, who Dalton initially expected to let go. British superstar Ben Ainslie joined and became Barker's trial-horse skipper.

Also back on board was Kevin Shoebridge, who had sailed with Dalton on *Lion New Zealand* and *Merit Cup*, but unlike Dalton, Shoebridge with his sailmaking background did make the cut for the 1987 New Zealand challenge America's Cup team and was part of

the crew of *KZ-7* in Fremantle.

Shoebridge sailed with Peter Blake on *Steinlager 2*, competing against the Dalton-skippered *Fisher & Paykel*. After he competed in the 1992 America's Cup aboard the radical *NZL-20*, their paths crossed again, with Shoebridge sailing with Dalton in the 1993–94 Whitbread on *New Zealand Endeavour*. Moving between America's Cup campaigns and round-the-world races, he was part of Team New Zealand to win the America's Cup in 1995. The pair came back together again on the Dalton-skippered *Merit Cup* for the 1997–98 Volvo Ocean Race finishing second overall in the nine-boat fleet.

Shoebridge skippered *Team Tyco* in the 2001–2002 Volvo Ocean Race, before joining the Kiwi professional sailing exodus to the challenger ranks for the 2003 America's Cup where he sailed with billionaire-backed US entry OneWorld in the Louis Vuitton Cup — being eliminated at the Semi-Final stage.

The long-time sailing buddies came together again at Emirates Team New Zealand for the 2007 America's Cup challenge, in a sailing and operations management role.

Shoebridge and Dalton offset and complement each other well. The aggressive Dalton has the grit and drive to scrap and succeed in the hurly-burly of sailing politics, sponsorship and fundraising. A former sailmaker, Shoebridge is more in the Blake mould — a soothing and calmer influence, with the skills to keep the engine of an America's Cup campaign ticking over, and ready to race.

The two were a familiar sight, alone together, in the bow of the team's main chase boat in Bermuda.

Matteo de Nora was one of the first people to step up after what was one of the greatest debacles in America's Cup and sailing history.

More important than his financial investment was his mentoring and advice to the team.

'He's the man I speak to every day of the week, whether we are together or on the phone across the hemispheres. He would give me advice, and sometimes it wasn't advice, it was an order,' Grant Dalton said introducing de Nora at the final media conference in Bermuda after Emirates Team New Zealand had achieved its third America's Cup win.

'Matteo invested knowing we had to be different. We had to have the right people who could think differently and knew what they were doing,' Dalton added.

'It is about catching opportunities,' de Nora explained in response to the next question. 'Team New Zealand won the Cup; I didn't win the Cup. And, when I met Grant I knew that we had an opportunity to get somewhere, and here we are. It took longer than we expected, but we got there, so it was mission accomplished. It is about the people I met and the people Grant has put together to make this team. It has been a winning team for several years. It was already a winning team in San Francisco and before that. We just got across the final line today. It has been a winning team for a long time.

'It isn't about money when you are talking about Team New Zealand, believe me,' he quipped when asked if his financial investment was money well spent.

Grant Dalton elaborated on Matteo de Nora's involvement and role in an interview with the *Sunday Star-Times* in February 2007, as the team prepared to leave before taking on Alinghi in the 32nd America's Cup.

'When I came on board after we lost the Cup in 2003, Team New Zealand had no money,

nothing, even before the government came to the party. I didn't think we would get through the first month, so I had to find someone to pay the electricity bill at the base, for example.

'I picked up the phone and rang Matteo [a supporter of Team New Zealand's 2003 campaign], and this bloke is the reason why we're now going to Valencia,' he said.

To say that Matteo de Nora has kept a low-profile in the three America's Cup campaigns is a huge understatement. While he is often present with the team, he stays well below the media radar and easily wandered unrecognised in the crowds of Emirates Team New Zealand fans in Bermuda, looking like just another Kiwi supporter.

De Nora's sport is offshore powerboat racing, competing on the European circuits in the 70s and 80s. Afterward, he moved across to trans-oceanic cruising and had the first of two superyachts built in New Zealand in 1993, before buying a property in the Bay of Islands.

In typical self-deprecating manner, de Nora tried to get away with telling the *Sunday Star-Times* that 'he owned an engineering firm that sold batteries'.

At the time the de Nora family business, founded in 1920, designed, manufactured and marketed sophisticated fuel cells in around 500 family-owned factories in Asia, Europe and South America.

His first involvement in the America's Cup was as a supplier of lightweight battery packs, expertise and a modest investment in the 2003 Team New Zealand campaign.

'But the moment I saw the mast snap in 2003, I knew I was going to get involved more,' he said.

'It broke my heart. I was in San Diego [when Team New Zealand won the Cup back in 1995] and was involved on a minor level in previous campaigns. But that's when the emotional attachment with the team started,' he said in the SST interview.

'I knew the team was better than that,' de Nora told the *Sunday Star-Times*.

Team New Zealand simply wouldn't exist without de Nora, Dalton said in a July 2017 interview with de Nora by NZME's Jane Phare.

Matched International America's Cup race yachts were used in the Louis Vuitton Pacific Series. Emirates Team New Zealand beat Alinghi in the Final. — RICHARD GLADWELL

Team NZ quite simply wouldn't exist without him, Dalton says. Many private benefactors have helped, including Sir Stephen Tindall, but de Nora is 'the glue'. He backed Dalton and the team at times when they faced many critics.

Apart from his considerable and ongoing financial contribution, amounting to millions of dollars over the years, Dalton says that de Nora became increasingly valuable from a management perspective and as a mentor.

Highly intelligent, he is one of those rare people who can 'unjumble thinking in your brain and lay you a plan and he can do it in a minute'.

De Nora likes things to be perfect, has a 'massive' memory and is immensely focused on detail, qualities that Dalton can relate to. That, and de Nora's values.

'He thinks very, very much like a Kiwi. He is hugely loyal. He believes in trust, that your word is your bond. He is a special human being.'

While the general public and ever-sceptical general media were very much a work in progress, the sponsor and marine industry support signed up, including Emirates Airlines as new naming rights sponsor for the team. Toyota, a major sponsor since the New Zealand America's Cup campaign in 1992, remained loyal. The New Zealand Government, persuaded about the benefits of the visibility and trade-show potential from an America's Cup in Europe, came in as an albeit controversial sponsor.

With the assistance of a $5 million loan (later repaid) by Alinghi's Ernesto Bertarelli, Dalton, ever a pragmatist, took a short-term success approach. He rebuilt the team using a series of pre-America's Cup regattas, known as Acts, staged by the new holders to build interest in the first America's Cup to be staged in Europe.

Good early performances helped. The Kiwis won Act 2 and placed a close second to the America's Cup champion, Alinghi, in Act 3. The Dalton-led team, now Emirates Team New Zealand, won the 2004 America's Cup Class World Championship.

In 12 months, the team had rekindled its self-belief and sponsor credibility. The fan support, however, was still a work in progress.

Emirates Team New Zealand shows her unusual bow, sailing against Team Shosholoza (RSA) in the 2007 Louis Vuitton Cup, Valencia, Spain. — Todd Niall

That racing success carried on through 2005 and 2006, leading into the 2007 America's Cup, and its preliminary Challenger Selection Series, the Louis Vuitton Cup. Emirates Team New Zealand, with Grant Dalton part of the sailing crew, got away to a slow start in the 32nd America's Cup Regatta sailed in Valencia, Spain. They lost three of the 10 races sailed in Round Robin 1, to lie third on the points table. Then they swept clean in Round Robin 2, winning all 10 races.

In the Semi-Finals, the Kiwis put away Spanish team Desafío Español 5–2, and then faced off against Italian Challenger Luna Rossa, skippered by Jimmy Spithill (of Australia) in the Louis Vuitton Final, winning that series 5–0. The series was much harder than the score indicated.

The scene was set for a rematch of the 2003 debacle in Auckland, except the roles of challenger and defender were reversed. To add to the intrigue, Russell Coutts, Alinghi's skipper in Auckland, had been sidelined after a falling out with team principal, Ernesto Bertarelli. Coutts was replaced with former world champion match racer Ed Baird, who had also been a Team New Zealand coach for the 1995 win in San Diego.

On board Alinghi was the backbone of Team New Zealand from 1995 and 2000, and Alinghi in 2003, Brad Butterworth, Murray Jones, Dean Phipps, Simon Daubney and Warwick Fleury. All three-time Cup winners, now looking for their fourth.

Since winning the America's Cup in Auckland, Ernesto Bertarelli had made a determined and successful effort to put the America's Cup on a very solid financial footing. The event managers America's Cup Management had ruffled many feathers along the way, and in the view of the challengers were playing an overly hard game.

That impression was probably what drove thousands of New Zealand supporters to travel to Valencia, from all around Europe and New Zealand. Labelled Camp Kiwi, they formed a vociferous fan base, urging on Emirates Team New Zealand, while the Swiss Defender, sailing in Spain, struggled to muster any real fan support.

Although *NZL-92* won the start of the first race, Alinghi crept away to win by 35 seconds, with most of that on the final run to the finish. It was clear that unlike 2003, the Kiwis had real spine and were going to be no pushover.

Those hopes were boosted in Race 2 when Barker staged a come-from-behind effort to win by a handy 28-second margin. That was the first time since the 1992 Cup that both teams were on the America's Cup leaderboard.

Emirates Team New Zealand took the third race, started in light and fluctuating winds, and punctuated by wild, gambling tactics and handling snafus. After at least three lead changes, Barker pulled 40 seconds out of his 2003 nemesis on the final run to win by 25 seconds.

As the Kiwi fans smelled blood, Alinghi bounced back with an end-to-end win, by the now regulation 30 seconds in Race 4, again sailed in light shifty wins. The needle with Alinghi and event organisers continued with a measurement incident when Alinghi apparently failed a test of whether their mainsail halyard lock could be released unassisted. The Kiwi team took the incident to the Jury Room, hoping to use video evidence to cost the Swiss the point for their race win, but lost in a majority verdict.

The sea breeze cracked in for Race 5, with

Barker winning the start and first beat, but a hole in the spinnaker on the first run escalated into a foredeck horror show, as at one stage the Kiwis had one blown spinnaker flying, another wrapped around the forestay, and the third trying to set. They dropped 38 seconds on the leg, regaining their composure on the final beat to chop Alinghi's margin back to 19 seconds. That put the score to 3–2 in favour of Alinghi.

Emirates Team New Zealand again led for the first two legs of Race 6, before allowing Alinghi to split away on the second beat and yet another lead change, easing away on the fourth leg and final run to win by 28 seconds.

With Alinghi on Match Point, Emirates Team New Zealand lost one of the most dramatic races in America's Cup history, after incurring a penalty at the end of the second windward leg (or beat).

Alinghi tactician Brad Butterworth called for a dial-down on *NZL-92*, as she tacked for the windward mark apparently leading but was the give-way boat. Butterworth got the Kiwis in his long-range sights, sprung the trap and got a penalty against his former team.

The drama continued as the wind began to drop away and become very patchy on the final run to the finish. Despite trailing, New Zealand got on the right side of a very big wind shift and ghosted towards the finish with a race-winning lead — except for her yet-to-be-performed penalty turn. Barker spun *NZL-92* just before the finish line, washing off all their speed, and had to slowly rebuild as Alinghi crawled to finish at the opposite end of the line. The initial margin was called 2 seconds, later reduced to just 1 second — and a dead heat to the home viewer.

Emirates Team New Zealand and Luna Rossa practise starting in AC72s off Takapuna Beach, March 2013. — RICHARD GLADWELL

Dalton described the atmosphere on board *NZL-92* as being 'like your heart has been dug out with a spoon'.

That narrowest of wins was sufficient for Alinghi to win what was a very closely fought match, and one which surprised most pundits. The fightback by Emirates Team New Zealand was remarkable, given the crew departures after their win in 2000, which set up their decimation in 2003.

Although bitterly disappointed at the outcome, on the positive side the team had been rebuilt, had new heart and self-belief and had regained their mana with the New Zealand sailing fans. Emirates Team New Zealand had re-established its sponsorship base, and as the Challenger had a healthy payout as its share of the surplus generated from Bertarelli's commercialisation of the 32nd America's Cup.

Team New Zealand's solid foundation then took what should have been a fatal hit.

A few weeks later, Golden Gate Yacht Club and the Larry Ellison-backed BMW Oracle Racing, which had been eliminated at the Semi-Finals stage of the 2007 Louis Vuitton Cup, lodged first a challenge with Alinghi's club Société Nautique de Genève (SNG) and then a complaint with the New York Supreme Court over SNG's choice of challenger for the 33rd America's Cup.

SNG had accepted a challenge from a newly formed Spanish club, Club Náutico Español de Vela (CNEV). The club had been in existence for just a few weeks and had never held a yacht race, let alone an annual regatta on an arm of the sea as required by the 19th-century Deed of Gift which controls the conduct of the America's Cup lodged by the original donors of the trophy with the New York Supreme Court.

CNEV was located in a small office in the Desafío Español base in Valencia. Quite why they were formed has never been explained. However, it seemed that it was an attempt to have a more unified relationship between the Defender and Challenger, as well as to give the next defence in Valencia more of a home-town feel.

The resulting legal arguments and numerous hearings and appeals kept the America's Cup on ice from July 2007 until February 2010. That is a very long period for a commercially based racing team to survive. They were the dark years for the other teams caught in billionaires' crossfire.

The sidebar story was that after a contract dispute with Bertarelli for the duration of the 2007 America's Cup cycle, his former skipper, Russell Coutts, was now a free agent and had been snapped up by BMW Oracle Racing and its backer, software tycoon Larry Ellison, as his skipper and CEO. That probably hardened Alinghi attitudes towards the San Francisco club.

As a stopgap measure, Louis Vuitton stepped in and backed a series of competitions involving the 2007 America's Cup teams sailing two matched pairs of International America's Cup Class yachts from teams involved in the Valencia regatta. The Louis Vuitton Pacific Series was staged in Auckland in February 2009, with 10 teams competing. Alinghi was a late entry, conditional on the dropping of a lawsuit against the Swiss team and America's Cup holders by Emirates Team New Zealand.

The Agreement between Emirates Team New Zealand and Alinghi was signed around 25 July 2007, three weeks after the conclusion of the 32nd America's Cup. It provided

The Commodore of Société Nautique de Genève hands over the America's Cup to the Golden Gate Yacht Club in February 2010. — RICHARD GLADWELL

certainty as to the future dates of America's Cup competitions to be held in 2009, and was backed by penalty clauses. On that basis, Emirates Team New Zealand had signed three key sponsors, Emirates Airlines, Toyota and the New Zealand Government.

At that time, Emirates Team New Zealand was clearly the kingmaker in the dispute between Alinghi and BMW Oracle Racing. In a protracted night of negotiation, Dalton was urged on the one hand by Bertarelli to enter under assured conditions, and on the other by Tom Ehman of BMW Oracle Racing to stay out of the game and force Bertarelli's hand.

Despite a lot of criticism, Dalton threw his lot in with Alinghi, secured the conditions he needed to get an America's Cup run in 2009, and put the reputation of Emirates Team New Zealand on the line for Alinghi. He had no option but to take a pragmatic approach. The

deal which got the America's Cup back on the rails more quickly was always the best one for New Zealand, regardless of the Protocol rules governing the conduct of the event.

Bertarelli, in turn, used the Kiwi entry many times to justify his actions, saying that the entry of a team of the standing of Emirates Team New Zealand was proof positive that his Protocol was not unreasonable.

The Kiwi lawsuit — handled by the same high-profile law firm that was representing Golden Gate Yacht Club — was designed to get everyone back on the water as soon as possible. The America's Cup siege between the two billionaires' respective teams had created collateral damage for Emirates Team New

Emirates Team New Zealand's Dean Barker, Grant Dalton, Kevin Shoebridge and Ray Davies ahead of the 2009 Louis Vuitton Pacific Series. — RICHARD GLADWELL

Zealand and other America's Cup teams. The agreement provided for an America's Cup to be sailed in 2009.

In a March 2008 interview Dalton did with Sail-World.com from New York, he seemed to accept that the 2009 date was no longer achievable. '2010 is a doable environment, and 2011 is more practical,' he said. The multi-challenger event contracted for 2009 was eventually sailed four years later in 2013.

In March 2008, the America's Cup stand-off resulted in the redundancy of 25 team members, cutting Emirates Team New Zealand down to 60 people, primarily sailing team and designers.

'This argument with Alinghi and related parties is completely commercial,' said Dalton. 'I get angry when I have to be involved in the redundancy of people who have worked for Team New Zealand for 15 years and were expecting their mortgage payment next month was also going to be from Team New Zealand because they have been re-employed. That makes me angry. That's not right.

'To a man, the guys have stayed completely loyal and stayed with us through what has been a difficult time for them. But they have to make a living as well.'

The Auckland-based Louis Vuitton Pacific Series used two of Team New Zealand's International America's Cup Class (IACC) boats and two from BMW Oracle Racing which were shipped to Auckland. The series, which was exhibition sailing at its very best, did recapture some of the glitz, glamour and drama of the series that had occurred in 2003 in Auckland. But it was not the same.

Emirates Team New Zealand salvaged some more home-town credibility with a win in the final series on the Waitemata with a 3–1 scorecard over their nemesis, Alinghi. The final day was sailed in torrid conditions — driving rain and a 25 kt-plus south-westerly breeze. More like winter off Cape Horn than summer on the Waitemata.

The series was the only one sailed in Auckland. Emirates Team New Zealand is an America's Cup racing team, not an events organiser. The commercially based team was not prepared to see its funds chewed up running sailing regattas involving two teams whose billionaire owners were still fighting each other in the New York Supreme Court to the detriment of the other 10 teams who were willing to compete — even under the Alinghi Protocol.

For the Kiwis, pragmatism overruled perfection. Any America's Cup was better than a perfect America's Cup. That pragmatic attitude extended to building a new boat and entering a team into the hot European TP52 racing circuit in 2009 and 2010. Skippered by Dean Barker and using their America's Cup crew, they won the circuit in both years, becoming the first team to win back-to-back titles in the seven-year history of the Audi Cup circuit.

Next target was an entry in the 2011–12 Volvo Ocean Race, with a Botin-designed Volvo Open 70 *Camper with Emirates Team New Zealand*. Skippered by Australian Chris Nicholson, the team included several of the America's Cup crew with round-the-world race experience. After an indifferent start in the opening legs, the team dug deep on the final three legs around the European coast and salvaged a highly credible second place overall in the 40,000-nautical mile race.

Meanwhile, the almost three-year battle in the New York State legal system had exhausted all available levels of appeal without a settlement between the protagonists that would enable a regular multi-challenger America's Cup to take place. Instead, the New York Supreme Court dictated that the default provisions of the Deed of Gift would apply, in the event the parties could not agree on conditions for the Match.

The practical effect of that decree was that the Match would be sailed off Valencia, Spain in early February 2010, during the European winter, in boats that were open design, provided they complied with the provisions of the Deed of Gift requiring them to be 'propelled by sails', constructed in the respective country of the challenging or defending club, and were within the minimum and maximum size on the load water line, specified in the Deed of Gift.

The protagonists heeded the lesson of the previous Deed of Gift Match sailed off San Diego in 1988 when the Defender, San Diego Yacht Club and their wingsailed 65-ft catamaran *Stars & Stripes*, trounced the bigger New Zealand Challenge's 90-ft LWL, 120-ft overall monohull *KZ-1*.

There were no technology constraints in the best-of-three match for the 33rd America's Cup. Everything was on the design table as the teams explored options that had never been fully tested on that scale in sailing, let alone developed under a tight time constraint. That set the scene for the 2013 and 2017 America's Cups, contested in wingsailed multihulls which continued to import aeronautical technology into the contest for the Auld Mug.

Both teams opted for 120-ft multihulls that were a maximum allowed length of 90 ft on the load water line. The Defender, Alinghi, chose a catamaran. The Challenger, BMW Oracle Racing, opted for a 90-ft LWL trimaran which had 90-ft beam (wide) and took 150,000 man-hours to build. Both yachts were initially sailed with 'soft' rigs — conventional masts and sails. After breaking their mast while training off San Diego, BMW Oracle Racing produced a 'hard' rig in the form of a 68-metre wingsail, the largest wing ever built, and more than twice the length of a Boeing 747 wing.

First showing for the wingsailed trimaran, on 11 November 2009, was viewed by backer Larry Ellison and hundreds of sailing fans via a Fox5 webcam mounted on a San Diego tower block. Watching her performance on webcams

BMW Oracle Racing's 120-ft wingsailed trimaran featured the largest wing (sail) ever constructed to win the 2010 America's Cup. — RICHARD GLADWELL

became a regular pastime.

Rumour was that Alinghi had looked at developing a similar wingsail, but had dismissed it on budgetary grounds.

The trimaran's first moves on the enclosed waters of San Diego Bay were impressive as she was gently put through her paces. Three weeks later the wingsailed Challenger was packed up and shipped to Valencia.

The 2010 technology race was a very comfortable fit with the resources of BMW Oracle Racing. Little was revealed before the start of the 33rd Match, but in the intervening days waiting for conditions suitable for racing, the true extent of the Challenger's technology was unveiled in a series of very frank and open media sessions.

Given that knowledge, the results on the water came as little surprise.

The racing in Valencia was held in the

winter, with the courses being set well offshore — sometimes taking an hour to reach travelling at 35 kts in a chase boat. The windchill factor was bitter. One night it snowed and when we looked back from the water in the morning there was a dusting of snow on the hills, with clear blue skies.

BMW Oracle Racing made a dramatic start in the first race, flying two of her three hulls in just 8 kts of breeze, as they rounded the Race Committee boat with her helmsman Jimmy Spithill holding right of way. He lined up *Alinghi 5* as they both entered the starting box ready for 5 minutes of clumsy manoeuvring in boats designed for speed not match-racing.

Alinghi, with owner Ernesto Bertarelli at the helm, was caught and penalised in a sensational start to the regatta. Five minutes later it was Spithill's turn for a faux pas, as the 90-ft trimaran *USA 17* was caught 'in irons' in sailing ship parlance. She sat stalled during a tack and was near-motionless for several minutes as Alinghi cleared her penalty and headed off up the 20-nautical mile first leg with a lead of 650 metres.

In one of the most remarkable scenes in sailing history, BMW Oracle Racing sorted their issues and set off in hot pursuit. After a few minutes, it was apparent that they were both higher and faster than the Swiss catamaran. Then *USA 17* dropped their jib and sailed even faster under wingsail alone. After 18 minutes of sailing, they caught and passed Alinghi and headed off for a 15 minute 28-second win on the two-leg 40-mile course.

The start of the second of the best-of-three

Signature moment of the 33rd America's Cup Match as BMW Oracle Racing spectacularly lifts off to enter the start of Race 1. — RICHARD GLADWELL

series got under way two days later on 12 February 2010. Both combatants kept clear of each other, and a more conventional race was sailed with the US Challenger showing some of her earlier speed advantage, but with Alinghi sailing a smarter first leg and with the benefit of a wind shift crossing ahead. Oracle had a small lead at the first mark but then lit the afterburner, showing the awesome power of the wingsail, on the next two reaching legs averaging almost 27 kts in the 7–8 kt breeze.

The race finished with both yachts showing navigation lights in the falling darkness, and with the Challenger 5 minutes 26 seconds ahead to go on to two wins in the best of three, winning the 33rd Match and taking the America's Cup back to the USA for the third time.

The new holder, Golden Gate Yacht Club, immediately accepted a challenge from Italy's Club Nautico di Roma represented by their team Mascalzone Latino, headed by shipping magnate Vincenzo Onorato, who negotiated a Protocol with the Golden Gate Yacht Club.

After three years of courtroom rhetoric, most pundits believed Golden Gate Yacht Club were the White Knights who could save and rejuvenate the America's Cup. GGYC held a live-streamed media conference in Rome's Musei Capitolini surrounded by some of Italy's most precious art treasures. Russell Coutts and Vincenzo Onorato set out a consultation process and timetable to set in place the foundation stones for the 34th America's Cup.

Golden Gate Yacht Club also commissioned separate design exercises for monohull and multihull options.

Fourteen teams submitted notices of entry, allowing them to compete in the preliminary America's Cup World Series, but two were declined, and nine progressively withdrew.

Unsurprisingly, the choices for the 34th America's Cup Class were for a wingsailed 72-ft catamaran, with the regatta to be staged in 2013, and a Protocol which contained many of the items over which GGYC had complained of for so long in the New York Supreme Court with SNG/Alinghi. Later the venue was predictably announced as San Francisco.

Having negotiated a Protocol, Club Nautico di Roma withdrew, with financial reasons being cited. In their place stepped the second yacht club to file a challenge, Kungliga Svenska Segelsällskapet (KSSS) or the Royal Yacht Club of Sweden, with their team Artemis Racing, led by Swedish oil billionaire Torbjörn Törnqvist, a keen and active competitive sailor notably in the RC44 class, co-designed by Russell Coutts.

The media success of the radical wingsailed catamarans was confirmed in mid-June 2011 when Russell Coutts pitchpoled a 45-ft (AC45) wingsailed catamaran in front of a media gathering in San Francisco. The images and video were splashed over the general media, and even financial journals, who previously were at best lukewarm about anything to do with the America's Cup. After that media take-up there was no doubt that an F1-type event on the water had been created.

After the 2010 Match in giant multihulls, most of the 12 potential teams felt, or soon realised, that playing catch-up was beyond them. However, they did compete in the preliminary America's Cup World Series, sailed in the one-design AC45 wingsailed catamarans.

Emirates Team New Zealand took a case to the International Jury over the involvement of teams who were clearly only going to be competing in the America's Cup World Series participating in the voting and decision-making process for the next America's Cup Match. They had their complaint upheld and the challenging teams involved shrank to just three — Artemis Racing, Emirates Team New Zealand and the Italian Luna Rossa.

The lead-up to the start of the 34th America's Cup Regatta was marked with numerous cases taken to the International Jury. Most involved the Challenger of Record and Defender sitting on one side of the table and challengers Luna Rossa and Emirates Team New Zealand sitting on the other.

The usual role of the Challenger of Record is to represent the view of the majority of the challengers against that of the Defender. Instead, Artemis Racing, the Challenger of Record, often took their own side, standing against the majority of challengers.

For their part, Emirates Team New Zealand and Luna Rossa had formed a partnership under which the New Zealand team sold the Italians a base design for an AC72 and the two teams worked up together with both boats being launched and sailed in Auckland during the summer of 2012–13. That relationship was taken to the International Jury by the Challenger of Record and Defender, with the five-person body clipping the wings of the cosy relationship, but not ruling it illegal.

Emirates Team New Zealand also hit on the design concept of being able to make the AC72

Emirates Team New Zealand take their first steps into the multihull world, sailing two SL33s in July 2011. — RICHARD GLADWELL

catamaran use its wingsail and considerable righting momentum to be able to lift out on foils. The breakthrough was unveiled to an incredulous sailing world in early September 2012, with the feature being copied across into the Luna Rossa design package.

Both Oracle Team USA and Artemis Racing complained to the International Jury that foiling wasn't allowed under the Protocol or Class Rule for the AC72, but the case was dismissed.

Unfortunately, the Kiwis had shown their hand too early, and the two other teams were able to modify designs and incorporate the foiling concept, with its crude control systems, into what had been intended as a displacement catamaran concept. That set the scene for a new and accelerated development direction, with the Kiwis holding the advantage of a head start.

In mid-October 2012, Oracle Team USA suffered a major setback. When caught in a rising breeze close to the Golden Gate Bridge, helmsman Jimmy Spithill bore away in a 33-kt gust and the Defender's first AC72 pitchpoled, and then broke up after being carried by the fast-ebbing tide out below the Golden Gate and deposited in the Pacific Ocean.

In a second incident in May 2013, just weeks before the start of the Challenger Selection, Artemis Racing suffered a structural failure in their first AC72 on its final sail, resulting in the death of a crew member and forcing a major revision of the safety and other rules for the regatta.

Regatta Director Iain Murray produced a list of 37 changes, most of which were agreed by the teams. One change was a lowering in maximum wind limit from 33 kts down to 23 kts. Emirates Team New Zealand had built and tested their boat for the top-end wind strength,

including sailing home from one test sail on the Waitemata as a tornado hit Auckland.

Oracle Team USA, on the other hand, had opted for a design which was much more aerodynamically efficient than the Kiwis' and Italians'. It is arguable, based on the experience with their first boat, whether OTUSA's second would have been able to sail at the top end of the initial wind range.

In consultation with the teams, Oracle Team USA plumped for a 20 kts maximum, while Emirates Team New Zealand went for 25 kts, and the middle figure of 23 kts was adopted. Unusually, the method of measuring wind strength was based on applying a tidal-correction factor from a computer model of the mid-course point in San Francisco Harbour and reducing or increasing the wind-strength maximum according to the dictates of the model. The system had never been used in an international sailing regatta previously and has never been since.

Emirates Team New Zealand easily won the Challenger Selection Series or Louis Vuitton Cup from Luna Rossa and Artemis Racing. Artemis were only able to sail their second boat in four races before being eliminated. Their campaign had by one estimate cost $1 million for every minute of sailing in the Louis Vuitton Cup.

After a protracted series of hearings and investigation by the International Jury, Oracle Team USA was fined $250,000, docked 2 points in the match and had crew and shore team suspended for varying periods after boat-

Racing AC72s, Emirates Team New Zealand powers over Oracle Team USA in the first leg of Race 1, 34th America's Cup in San Francisco. — RICHARD GLADWELL

measurement irregularities which had occurred in four of the America's Cup World Series lead-up regattas and had no direct bearing on the Match itself.

In the 34th America's Cup Match, the New Zealanders had a clear speed edge over the Defender, particularly upwind, and won the first three races by healthy margins. Oracle Team USA took the fourth by just 8 seconds after both boats fell off their foils, but for the first time Oracle was able to hold the Kiwis out to windward. The boats hit 40 kts plus in the final fast downwind in white water past Alcatraz, with Oracle Team USA taking their first victory.

The San Francisco waterfront was packed along its length with fans to watch the racing in the 34th America's Cup, September 2013. — RICHARD GLADWELL

There followed a lay day which Oracle Team USA spent on the water sailing in fresh winds, and Emirates Team New Zealand stayed ashore, preferring to work on their boat.

In Race 5, Oracle Team USA won the start after stitching up opposition skipper Dean Barker with some aggressive tactics. Although they led around the second mark, a tactical and boat-handling blunder by Oracle allowed the Kiwis to take the lead and win by over a minute. That put the New Zealanders on 5 points and had they won Race 6 set down for that afternoon, Emirates Team New Zealand was set to reach their required 9 points in just two more race days.

Oracle Team USA clearly had to play for time. Their performance data would have shown that in terms of boat speed they were slowly closing the gap on the Kiwis. Also, with the tide set

to change direction for the following week of racing, under the wind-strength model used, maximum wind limits would be reducing, and there was a good chance of only one race being sailed per day instead of the scheduled two.

In a cunning use of the rules, Oracle Team USA called a time out before Race 6, using a rule that was intended to allow a boat to repair damage, but which didn't specify under what circumstances it could be called into play. That, coupled with a scheduled lay day the next day, 11 September, gave Oracle Team USA a good break to reassess and regroup.

One of the changes was to bring their trial-horse skipper, four-time Olympic Gold medallist in the singlehanded Finn class, Ben Ainslie (Great Britain), into the afterguard, replacing tactician and San Francisco local John Kostecki, who appeared to be suffering a loss of form.

When racing resumed, the Kiwis took two wins from Races 6 and 7, to move to 6 points, and would probably have been on 7 points and been just one day's racing away from victory had Oracle not called their time out two days before.

Along with boat-speed gains, the new afterguard of the relentless match racer Jimmy Spithill, Australian Tom Slingsby (2012 Olympic Gold medallist) and Ben Ainslie, Oracle Team USA was beginning to gel nicely.

On the water, it was apparent that it was taking longer and longer for Emirates Team New Zealand to break through the Defender. The issue culminated in Race 8 when the Kiwis were forced to tack, but without sufficient hydraulic pressure to drive the wingsail shaping, and they came within half a degree of a capsize. That error gave Oracle Team USA their second win of the regatta and a zero points score (wiping out the 2 points deducted by the International Jury).

Emirates Team New Zealand regrouped and led the second race of the afternoon and looked set to go on to 7 points when the wind alarm was triggered on the Race Committee boat, and racing stopped while the Kiwis were comfortably ahead off Alcatraz, halfway up the third leg. That was the first of five races either postponed or abandoned due to wind limits being exceeded in the second week with the change in tidal direction. None were lost in the first seven days.

Claims made after the regatta that Grant Dalton had declined the opportunity to race on Monday, 16 September simply don't stack up.

A review of the governing documents showed that 16 September was never in the schedule as a race or reserve day. This is confirmed by an Oracle Team USA media release of 15 September which read: 'With no racing scheduled for Monday, Oracle team USA will spend part of the day training on the water. Racing resumes on Tuesday . . . '

The wind on 16 September was strong and even stronger the next race day (17 September) with a peak gust of 32 kts recorded. No racing took place on the 17th, and Emirates Team New Zealand won the only race able to be sailed on 18 September by just 15 seconds.

From there Oracle Team USA effected the changes in tactics and sailing technique that enabled them to come back into the Match. One of these was to deepen the camber in the wingsail to the same depth as that of the New Zealanders, allowing more power out of a tack with a lower angle, before flattening the wingsail as they got foiling upwind and came back up to a more efficient course. Aside from their poor initial tactical decisions, Oracle Team USA had gone into the Match with a lot of untapped potential which they were able to draw out given they had the time.

In the final week, Oracle had perfected their ability to consistently foil upwind, which coupled with their more aerodynamic hull and platform, meant reduced drag and a speed edge that the Kiwis could not match.

'We made a lot of changes on the boat; the boys sailed it quite differently,' Larry Ellison explained once the 34th America's Cup was back in his kitbag.

'We decided our VMG [velocity made good] was better when we put the bow down going to windward. We put the bow down and went fast, rather than sailing higher and slower. We did a lot of other things as well. We increased the horsepower of the boat, but I'm not going to go into details of exactly what we did,' he added.

With Oracle Team USA's newly found boat-speed advantage over the Kiwis, it was just a matter of repeating the performance and counting down the races.

Emirates Team New Zealand won their last race on 18 September and had the start of the second race for the day blown up when a wind limit was exceeded. The following week the tide turned again, and wind limits increased from a low of 19.9 kts the week before to 24.5 kts. No racing was lost in the final week, because of the wind limit being exceeded.

Three months earlier I had looked at the race schedule and formed the opinion that if the

---

Emirates Team New Zealand had the edge over Oracle Team USA in the first week of the 34th America's Cup, San Francisco. — RICHARD GLADWELL

regatta was still running at 18 September, then Emirates Team New Zealand would lose, and that was the day I booked my flight home. Leaving was hard, but that day proved to be the last win for New Zealand in the 34th America's Cup.

The New Zealanders' one hope was a light-weather race, where the wind stayed at 10 kts. Regatta Director Iain Murray commented after the race that the teams were all made very aware that they would be unable to complete the course in 10 kts of wind.

Oracle had calculated that the crossover for not requiring the large Code Zero jib was 11 kts, and made the bold call of not carrying the sail and its gear, including the bowsprit. That lightened the boat and reduced aerodynamic drag to assist foiling — particularly upwind. After that, it was all Oracle Team USA until they won their next eight races to take them to the required 11 races, and Golden Gate Yacht Club successfully defended the America's Cup.

The series was the longest ever in America's Cup history at 19 races and it covered almost a three-week period.

At the final media conference, skipper Dean Barker said he only really felt the regatta was beginning to slip away the previous day.

'That was the first time we felt we had a bit on. In the second race yesterday, we led around the bottom mark and watched Oracle sail around us and sail away into the distance on the upwind which had been our strength.

'Today we went in with the attitude that we were going to prepare as well as we possibly could, make sure we won the start, got around Mark 1 in front, get around that bottom gate and see what we could do. But, again, we saw how dominant Oracle have become upwind. It is very difficult to accept and a tough pill for us to swallow.'

Dalton reflected: 'I have slept better the last couple of days than I had a week ago because I sensed that something was going on. The upwind deltas changed by about a minute and a half in a week and a half. So that is a huge improvement that they have made. We had a bottom end in one of our tacks today of 14 knots — a month ago we were bottoming at 10 or 11 knots. So, we've improved a huge amount as well. In the end, we weren't quick enough.

'In Valencia, in 2007 we got up 2–1, but we weren't anywhere near as strong as we are here. This is a completely different team here in terms of its strength.

'After Valencia, we felt we peaked for the Louis Vuitton Final. This time we were very conscious that we hit our peak on Day 1 of the America's Cup, and we won the first two races.

'Certainly, here we plateaued relative to Oracle, but they were trying to learn how to sail their boat at the beginning of the regatta and while we were at our peak.

'We have improved quite a bit, the numbers are irrelevant now, but we didn't have as far to go as Oracle. That was never the intention because we wanted to be going as fast as we could on Day 1. If you look at our speed now compared to the Louis Vuitton Final we are massively faster than we were then.

'But their rate of improvement was greater because they had more in the tank, plus a lot of disruptions coming into the Match.

'My life finishes now. In terms of my future — I haven't given it any thought at all.'

Those closing comments set the scene for what was to come at the start of the 35th America's Cup cycle and Emirates Team New Zealand's four-year build-up for Bermuda.

Chapter 3

Aftermath of 2013

The inevitable happened on the afternoon of 25 September 2013, on San Francisco Bay.

Oracle Team USA won the 19th and final race of the 34th America's Cup.

Jimmy Spithill had a grin on his face that spread all the way to his native Australia. He'd just achieved one of the great comebacks of international sport and won 11 races to Emirates Team New Zealand's eight.

The body language at the post-match media conference said a lot. Spithill and Oracle Team USA, including owner Larry Ellison, were jubilant. Oracle Corporation's annual conference for key staff and clients was running in San Francisco for the final week of the America's Cup, and the events on the water couldn't have provided a better backdrop and stronger subliminal message to those attending.

Emirates Team New Zealand skipper Dean Barker faces a media conference at the 34th America's Cup, San Francisco. — RICHARD GLADWELL

Ellison, viewed by many in San Francisco as a somewhat Machiavellian character, fielded a barrage of questions from the gathered media and was clearly enjoying himself and swatting away any acerbic angles as the US media tried to trap him with their lengthy carefully framed speeches masquerading as questions. When the interrogators strayed away from the victory and into his personal life and assets, the seventh richest man in the world told the questioner the answer was in a recent unauthorised joint biography, *The Billionaire and the Mechanic*.

On the other side of the table, the Emirates Team New Zealand crew were in varying stages of discomposure. CEO Grant Dalton was more relaxed, having seen the inevitable a week out, and managed to give some witty answers to a couple of questions engaging in the gallows-type humour for which Kiwi sailors are renowned when explaining away an awkward loss.

His skipper, Dean Barker, was clearly dazed and very upset by the turn of events. Principal

Matteo de Nora was serious but accepting of what had transpired, while tactician Ray Davies was his usual chipper self.

Just over a week later on the day after arriving back in New Zealand, Dean Barker was interviewed on the prime-time news show *Campbell Live*. It was an eerie setting with heavily subdued lighting and shuttered windows as though they were in a funeral parlour. The side light contrasted the angles on Barker's face. He still appeared to be in a state of confused shock, talking quietly in a very flat monotone.

Three days later at the official welcome

home for the losing team, the sign held by fans at the top of the ASB Building on the Viaduct waterfront said it all.

'You won our hearts.'

Despite the inclement weather, there was a big turnout — maybe not on the scale of the 1995 victory, but it took Barker and Dalton 20 minutes to force their way through the crowd gathered in Shed 10 in downtown Auckland.

There it was a much more relaxed and happier Dean Barker. 'Today more than any time before I am proud to be a New Zealander', reiterating the point made to John Campbell three days earlier that the high point of the campaign was the support from New Zealand.

Fans at Shed 10 ran the full gamut of emotions — pride, grief, and a huge sense of unity born out of a shared common experience

Crowds of Auckland fans turned out to welcome Emirates Team New Zealand home at a waterfront parade. — RICHARD GLADWELL

in the company of complete strangers.

The political backer of the team, Minister for Economic Development Steven Joyce, who had been cynical about the America's Cup campaign before he went to San Francisco, was now a strong supporter. He'd seen the leverage New Zealand companies were able to generate from interacting with much larger organisations in the same industry in the technological hub of San Francisco and the west coast of the USA.

Joyce told the fans and team: 'This country and this government stands ready to be part of the next America's Cup. Bring us a proposal, and we will work with you on it.'

Then followed a parade in front of tens of thousands of fans gathered around waterfront vantage points as the team showed off the Louis Vuitton Cup, which they had won in 1995 and 2007, before heading off to the Royal New Zealand Yacht Squadron for a club reception.

Three weeks later Joyce announced an interim government investment of $5 million towards the team's challenge for the 35th America's Cup, saying the bridging funding would enable the team to retain designers, sailors, support crew and administration for the next challenge.

Government investment in Emirates Team New Zealand is a relatively recent phenomenon. Up until the 2000 America's Cup Defence in Auckland, the New Zealand Government had struggled to really leverage off the event without becoming a formal sponsor. For its part, Team New Zealand could only really open the door for sponsors and suppliers under strict agreements governing the value given and received for varying levels of investment. The government's involvement was more in parallel activities to promote tourism and similar but with no direct connection to the team. The same applied in 2003 for the attempt at a second defence.

But the staging of the America's Cup in Valencia offered little in the way of parallel marketing opportunities. You were either part of the America's Cup, via the event or a team, or you were not.

Under the Labour Government, there was a mood to be involved,

'You won our hearts' was the theme of the homecoming parade around the Auckland waterfront with fans crowding every vantage point. — RICHARD GLADWELL

with Prime Minister Helen Clark being a strong supporter along with Minister Trevor Mallard. To be involved meant coming aboard as a sponsor, and getting visibility ashore and afloat, with the ability to run trade and tourism exhibitions ashore, flying in VIPs, and encouraging New Zealand companies to do the same around the America's Cup Village.

Even though they were unsuccessful in winning the 32nd America's Cup as the final Challenger left standing, Emirates Team New Zealand received a healthy share of the surplus from the Valencia event which was projected to be around NZ$48 million but was later published at over NZ$100 million. The distribution formula was for 10 per cent of the surplus going to the event organisers, 45 per cent to Alinghi as the Defender, and with the remaining 45 per cent distributed among the other teams according to how long they had managed to stay in contention.

The amount received by the Challenger in the Match, Emirates Team New Zealand, was reported at $14 million. America's Cup Management had even gone so far as to close the books early and bring the payout forward, so teams had a sound financial basis to carry them through until sponsorship taps started flowing for the 33rd America's Cup.

Those funds, and much more, were instead used to survive the six-year stand-off between Ernesto Bertarelli and Larry Ellison, as they battled each other through the New York Supreme Court, before having a court-ordered Match between two 120-ft multihulls, and before looking to what would happen for the 34th America's Cup, three years hence.

There was no such surplus payout from the America's Cup in San Francisco. Further, it seemed that Emirates Team New Zealand had bet the house on winning the America's Cup, and hadn't considered their financial survival beyond that point.

In sailing, Dalton is widely acknowledged as having an ability to attract funding and investment that is second to none. His leaving Emirates Team New Zealand at this critical time would have been more than a body blow.

Grant Dalton left New Zealand and returned in mid-December after two and a half months away, which included looking up sponsorship and investment opportunities to fund the team.

'We had poured everything into it over the past three years — never thinking past the last race — and there is a big void. The support at home has been very humbling,' Barker said in a Radio New Zealand interview.

'Now is still a time to regather, and look forward to the next event. We are not certain for the next event. We still have to wait for the next rule, or Protocol, which should be March or April next year. We need a lot of aspects of that to be favourable for our sponsors to be able to make a strong case for them to be back and involved in the team.'

For all Dalton's lifting of European financial rocks, there was not a lot to be had, particularly without any indication of an event, dates, class of boat and venue, plus the all-important television coverage plan.

The answers to those questions are vital to any commercially based professional America's Cup team, and they didn't start coming via the media until eight months later. Later Dalton claimed they never even got so much as an email for a year from the organisers of the next America's Cup.

Barker continued. 'I was up in Europe with

Grant Dalton recently, meeting with a number of different sponsors. They love the team and the values that go with it. They would very much like to be involved again, but they cannot commit until they know where it is and the timing.'

The New Zealand media never got over the recovery by Oracle Team USA. The Kiwi hacks could see their team was 8–1 up with potentially eight races left in the regatta, but if they had looked at the real win–loss situation, the score was 8–3 and after the fourth day of racing Oracle was winning as many or more races than Emirates Team New Zealand on a daily basis. In other words, the Kiwis were being hauled back, and it was just a matter of

whether the Defender had the time to overtake the Challenger.

When Oracle skipper Jimmy Spithill started his sledging of Dean Barker and the New Zealand team midway through the San Francisco regatta, some of the Kiwi media picked up on this theme, catching the defensive Barker in a pincer movement of hostile and supposedly friendly fire.

In San Francisco, after the main media conference was over, Emirates Team New Zealand would hold informal media scrums. They were most illuminating, with quite different stances being taken by the Kiwi team to those which they had taken a few minutes earlier up the other end of the room. Barker just dismissed Spithill's taunts as 'Jimmy being Jimmy' and 'I don't pay any attention to them'.

'It is fair to say that I haven't caught up over

Dean Barker (right) listens as Oracle Team USA's Jimmy Spithill responds to a media conference question with Tom Slingsby. — RICHARD GLADWELL

a beer with him [Jimmy Spithill], and I don't intend to either,' he told Radio New Zealand in mid-December, just under three months after San Francisco.

'I have a healthy respect for Spithill's sailing ability and everything else. People can think what they like about the mind games. I have been around the [America's Cup] game for quite a while, and you have to deal with a lot of pressure at times and the press conferences are exactly that — an opportunity for people to say what they think. We were very happy going into the finals and the Cup itself.

'The momentum started to swing well before it was 8–1, but they [Oracle] just kept on making mistakes. As the event went on, they made fewer mistakes and got better performance and that translated into results. There certainly wasn't a moment in a press conference when we threw in the towel and rolled over.'

The seeds were sown at the media conferences and they germinated into weeds during the eight months before the first edition of the new Protocol was published.

The sideline analysis soon began in New Zealand, particularly on talkback where they are not interested in facts, just an angle, and continued with the theme of Barker being a three-time loser, and why continue? Other themes included claims about the amounts team members were being paid; whether the government should be investing in a sports team (forgetting that Team New Zealand in its three renditions was the shop window for a $1.5 billion-a-year marine industry), plus the call for complete and open accountability of not just the government investment but indeed all the team's financial records.

Team New Zealand provided an infinite

variety of angles, and for talkback they were the gift that kept on giving.

The 'Barker Bashers' of course stayed clear of the facts over his track record. Some quick research showed that as helmsman (with Deed of Gift Matches excluded), Russell Coutts has helmed the most race wins in recent Cup Match history with 14 race wins, while Dennis Conner, Dean Barker and James Spithill all had 11 race wins. Ed Baird (Alinghi helmsman for the 2007 America's Cup) had five wins and John Bertrand of *Australia II* fame had four wins.

The reality was that Barker was in second place on the leaderboard and in some very good company. Only two of that group — Coutts and Barker — had won the ISAF Youth Singlehanded World Championships. (The last time any of them could be measured at the same age in the same class and same competition. Barker won Gold and Silver medals from the event, as has Ben Ainslie, the only two sailors to do so.) Russell Coutts has won three ISAF World Match Racing Championships as a helmsman. Ed Baird has one World Match Racing Championship win.

While Oracle Team USA had two America's Cup wins, even at that point Emirates Team New Zealand was still the most successful team in America's Cup history, a fact also overlooked by the Barker Bashers.

Ducking the friendly fire, the Kiwi team was gearing up and making some very deep-seated changes.

The first of these came early in the New Year of 2014. At a media conference at their Auckland base, in mid-January, Emirates Team New Zealand announced the signing of 2013 49er World and European Champions and 2012 Olympic Silver medallists, Peter Burling and

Blair Tuke. The move had been signalled for some time when Emirates Team New Zealand's CEO Grant Dalton first said that the team would campaign two AC45s in future America's Cup World Series.

The duo was also awarded 2013 New Zealand Sailors of the Year. They also won the inaugural Red Bull Youth America's Cup in a Yachting New Zealand-backed NZL Sailing Team, sailing in matched AC45s.

Burling and Tuke had been sailing together in the Olympic 49er class since 2009, and remarkably the 2016 Olympics was Burling's third Olympic Regatta at the age of 25. He sailed as a crew in the 2008 Olympics in Qingdao, at just 17 years old, and won his first Open World Championship at the age of 15.

The announcement of Burling and Tuke being on board signalled the new, informal relationship between Emirates Team New Zealand and the sport's national body, Yachting New Zealand, which had been lacking for many years.

Speaking at the soon-to-be-demolished Emirates Team New Zealand base, Grant Dalton made it clear that the organisation needed to grow and change.

'We came up short last time,' he said. 'We have to develop, we want to bring in new talent, and where possible we want to bring in Kiwi talent — particularly into the sailing team. There's no better talent in the country at present than Blair and Peter,' he added, making all the right noises.

Dalton was quick to point out that while

Burling/Tuke congratulate Nathan Outteridge and Iain Jensen on winning their Gold medals at the 2012 Olympics in Weymouth. The situation would be reversed at the 2016 Olympics, and the two crews fought out the Louis Vuitton Challenger Final in Bermuda in June 2017. — RICHARD GLADWELL

Emirates Team New Zealand skipper Dean Barker was a no-show at the media session, that was because Barker was still away with his family, up north, on holiday. Later he disclosed that Barker would be part of a new executive group to take the major decisions within Emirates Team New Zealand, rather than all decisions falling primarily on Dalton's shoulders, by design or default, as happened in the 34th America's Cup.

Key members of that new group were Dalton, Kevin Shoebridge (Chief Operating Officer), Nick Holroyd (Head Designer), Glenn Ashby

(Sails), and Dan Bernasconi (Performance Analysis). (Just over a year later, Barker and long-standing design head Nick Holroyd would have left to be part of a new Challenger, SoftBank Team Japan.)

Dalton said that one of the mistakes that was made in San Francisco was that the team closed into a 'very process-focused environment. We weren't able to respond quickly enough, because of that.'

He added: 'I've also got to take a good look at myself, too. There is so much experience in the organisation that the way we make decisions needs to be a little bit smarter.'

At the time, it was expected that Barker would take on a joint skipper and Sailing Director role, with the actual boat helmsman's position, and all

Peter Burling and Blair Tuke mid-fleet during the early stages of racing in the 49er class at the 2012 Olympic Regatta, Weymouth. — RICHARD GLADWELL

others, being contested within the team by the joint AC45 programme, starting in 2015.

The team had been shrunk from around 100 in San Francisco to just 29 people — of which about seven team members were current sailors. In what was to be a very significant comment, Dalton made it clear that the team would look towards Yachting New Zealand's High Performance Programme to take up more of the talent development load, ensuring that the team had a strong future from the two talent development streams.

Yachting New Zealand CEO David Abercrombie noted that the new relationship provided the means for Olympic sailors to make a living as professionals in the sport, extending their ability to stay in the sport — both in Olympic programmes and other professional sailing events. A physiotherapist, Abercrombie himself was formerly with BMW Oracle Racing in its earlier America's Cup campaigns. He joined Yachting New Zealand in late 2011.

For its design and engineering talent, the team already had a strong relationship with University of Auckland's School of Engineering and the Yacht Research Unit. With the availability of Prime Minister's Scholarships, via Yachting New Zealand plus other educational funding, there was a strong incentive for young sailors to pursue university education programmes,

Grant Dalton (right) introduces new signings, Olympic Silver medallists Peter Burling (left) and Blair Tuke (centre), January 2014. — RICHARD GLADWELL

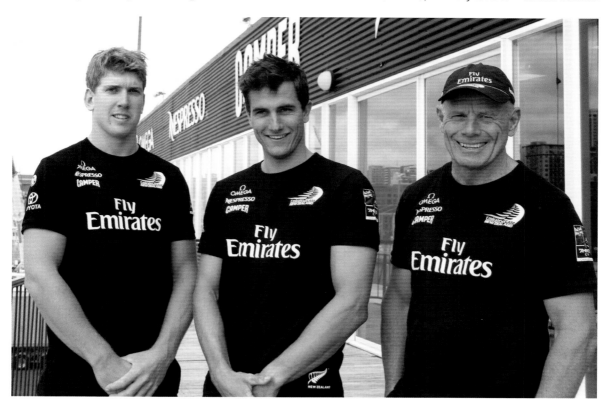

often in engineering.

At the time of joining Team New Zealand, Burling was about halfway through an engineering degree at Auckland.

Several sailors from the Yachting New Zealand Youth programmes, under the tutelage of Harold Bennett, had gone on to successful America's Cup careers.

Later Dalton revealed that both Tuke and Burling had received offers from other America's Cup teams, but said they would have been 'nuts' to go offshore at this stage of their sailing careers.

The 2016 Olympic campaign remained the primary focus for the then 49er World Champions and the America's Cup commitments, both sailing the Cup race boats and on the America's Cup World Series sailed in foiling AC45s, were worked into both programmes.

Tuke and Burling went on to win every 49er regatta except one in the four-year build-up in the Olympic skiff ahead of the Rio Olympics, winning the Gold Medal at Rio. Along the way, Burling won the 2015 foiling Moth Championships, sailed in Melbourne.

All told, four of the six regular America's Cup sailing crew in Bermuda came from the NZL Sailing Team and of the nine listed for sailing each day, five were Olympic medallists, covering three sports.

Another key change in the team was the introduction of a new board of directors. One of the areas of media concern about the team and the injection of government money was that externally it appeared to be a private fiefdom of Dalton and his mates.

The new and expanded Board was a condition of any additional investment by New Zealand Trade and Enterprise into the team and future America's Cups, or other related sailing activities, and the Board was to be acceptable to the Minister for Economic Development, Steven Joyce. The retiring chairman, Gary Paykel, a long-time mentor of Grant Dalton, made the announcement.

The expanded five-person Board was to be led by Dr Keith Turner, a former chief executive and experienced company director, who would be chairman. Among other directorships in New Zealand and Australia, Turner was then chairman of Fisher & Paykel Appliances Limited.

Others joining were long-time Team New Zealand supporter, philanthropist and businessman Sir Stephen Tindall, who was founder and director of The Warehouse Group, a major New Zealand retail chain. After Tauranga-based Keith Turner resigned in May 2015, Tindall took over as chairman.

Others joining the Board included Greg Horton, one of the founding directors of Harmos Horton Lusk, an Auckland-based specialist corporate legal advisory firm.

Another was Tina Symmans, who had more than 25 years' experience in advising companies, most particularly in the fields of strategic communications and corporate and government relations.

Recently retired Bob Field had 30 years as managing director and chair of Toyota New Zealand. He had been closely involved with Team New Zealand for 25 years, over six successive America's Cup campaigns, as a sponsor, an advisor and a mentor for the team.

Reporting to the Board was a six-person Executive Committee taking the major operational decisions comprising Dalton, Kevin Shoebridge, Nick Holroyd, Glenn Ashby, Dean

Barker and Dan Bernasconi.

The Board's immediate tasks were to review the Protocol when it became available, assess the possibility of mounting a credible challenge from New Zealand and prepare a business case for the New Zealand Government.

The Board met for the first time on 7 April 2014, and its impact was immediately discernible. Seven weeks later Emirates Team New Zealand Chairman Dr Keith Turner announced that the team had reached the point where it had the confidence to mount a challenge for the 35th America's Cup. The team had secured sufficient private and sponsorship funding to proceed to the next stage without needing government funding during this period.

'Now, with the assistance of long-time supporters Sir Stephen Tindall, Matteo de Nora and other private donors and sponsors, we are delighted to be able to say that we are funded through to late this year,' Turner said in a media statement released by the team.

On 7 August 2014, at the club's Annual General Meeting, outgoing Commodore Steve Burrett announced that the challenge would go ahead. Entries closed with the Golden Gate Yacht Club the following day (NZT).

The Royal New Zealand Yacht Squadron had been involved with all but two of New Zealand's America's Cup campaigns since 1987, winning at San Diego in 1995 and successfully defending at Auckland in 2000, before losing in 2003. RNZYS has won the Louis Vuitton Cup awarded to the winner of the Challenger Selection Series in 1995, 2007, 2013 and 2017.

It's a record second to none.

Emirates Team New Zealand Board members help bless Emirates Team New Zealand's AC50 in the pouring rain, February 2017. — RICHARD GLADWELL

SPORT

CRAIG'S LIST
NEW SPIN
STAR CHASES
CONTRACT
/ **P6**

THE PAIN IN SPAIN

WORLD CUP ACTION / P6-7

Flops, frolics and insults dominate Brazil 2014
- Chile are cheats say Socceroos
- Messi lies in wait
- World Cup holders devastated

MARK REASON
WHY I WANT
TIGER BACK
/ **P9**

Team NZ $6m and counting

By **SIMON PLUMB**
Twitter: @simonplumbffx

TEAM NEW Zealand boss Grant Dalton has managed to raise $6million over the last week – but could yet need to find another $3m before the month is out to remain in the America's Cup.

Dalton has also expressed frustration over the handling of Friday's Auckland press conference, saying portrayals he issued government with a funding ultimatum were not what was intended and it has only strained the political environment while the clock ticks.

The board of TNZ reconvenes tomorrow, including director and top entrepreneur Sir Stephen Tindall flying back into the country in the morning, to continue discussions on how the syndicate can finish tackling its potentially terminal financial situation – facing a deadline of just 14 days before their money runs out.

While timing of a $3m entry fee complicates the financials, as it stands TNZ effectively requires $5m to survive to December and an additional $6m to see them through to the end of February 2015.

Dalton has now revealed he has found commercial and private commitments, including from new investors, for $6m of that $11m total – an impressive achievement in the last seven days.

"In a week we have found $6m of funding ourselves, that is absolutely correct," Dalton told the *Sunday Star-Times* last night.

Economic Development Minister Steven Joyce has also suggested that in the short-term, government is prepared to pump in around another $2m of public money but TNZ must first meet the difference and have the cash ready. However, the relationship between TNZ and both the government and the public has been aggravated.

Joyce reacted to Dalton on Friday, quickly arranging his own press conference in response to reportage on TNZ after it was claimed Dalton had issued government with an ultimatum amounting to: 'give us more funding, or watch us die'.

Dalton says the TNZ press conference was not even called to discuss government funding, but instead to discuss the newly unveiled, and revised, protocol for the 2017 America's Cup – and crucially, to convey that a Kiwi victory was more realistic than had first been portrayed.

Dalton has also put his own hands up, acknowledging he should have known questioning about government funding would be fielded.

"I'm embarrassed in the extreme that it went in that [funding] direction, frankly we should have anticipated, that but didn't," he said. "The claim of an ultimatum was absolutely not what was intended – it's pretty obvious doing so would only make things harder.

"The first 40 minutes of the press conference discussed the protocol, it's a shame the majority of what was reported though was on questions which came after that about government funding."

Dalton said he is confident TNZ are in their best-ever commercial position long-term and that short-term problem is not the backing itself, but immediate cash flow. Dalton said a bank loan remains on the table, only it's not certain what assets TNZ has to secure such an agreement against.

ALL BLACKS	ENGLAND
28	27

Big Ben strikes: All Blacks matchwinner Ben Smith was in scintillating form in his home stadium last night, regularly splitting the England defence and pulling off the try-saving tackle of the year.

LANCASTER'S BOMBERS

Stuart Lancaster's England side bombed their opportunity to explode the All Blacks' aura last night after a devastating 20-minute spell in the second half sealed a series win for New Zealand in Dunedin

LIAM NAPIER: WHY THE TUILAGI EXPERIMENT BACKFIRED / P2
MARC HINTON: ALL BLACKS FIRE WHEN IT MATTERS / P3 / **PHIL GIFFORD: BEN SMITH'S MAGNIFICENT PERFORMANCE / P3**

Chapter 4

Black Friday

There's a long-standing joke between Cup veterans that an America's Cup campaign is three years of meetings followed by a boat race. Many times in the next three years the Team New Zealand management would be wishing it was that simple. The quiet life would be eluding them for some time.

With no sign of the Protocol for the 35th America's Cup in sight, Emirates Team New Zealand CEO Grant Dalton confirmed in a mid-April 2014 TV interview that the funding advance from the New Zealand Government would run out in June 2014, or in just over two months.

Appearing on the evening news show *Campbell Live*, Dalton nodded in confirmation of a statement by John Campbell that the team coffers would be empty at the end of June 2014. To survive beyond that date the team would be relying on the generosity of private backers. 'We won't see any significant sponsorship money this year,' Dalton told Campbell. 'You can't make it out of this year with sponsors — you never do,' he added.

Dalton confirmed they had offers on the table from some of their existing sponsors, despite not having a Protocol, or venue, for the 35th Cup announced. He pointed out that the next America's Cup was expected to be just as expensive as the last despite all the talk of cost cutting. However, the team was hamstrung by the lack of very basic information — which was required if the team was to be able to make a pitch to past and potential sponsors.

When pushed that this would surely be a given in the new Cup equation, Dalton quipped: 'Don't count on it — this is the America's Cup!'

At that stage, there were still four locations on the table: San Francisco, Chicago, San Diego and Bermuda.

Both Dalton and Barker confirmed that their relationship was tight, despite comments

---

Team New Zealand takes lead story in the *Sunday Star-Times* after the Black Friday media massacre, June 2014. — Fairfax Media

by others outside the team that someone else would be leading the team going into the 35th America's Cup.

Dalton stressed that before they could even look at their chances of winning the event, they had to get over the immediate money hurdle. That task was being made no easier by the two parties responsible for negotiating the Protocol for the next America's Cup — Hamilton Island and Golden Gate yacht clubs. The process had been running for over six months, and all indications were that it was a long way from a conclusion. 'Don't hold your breath'

was the comment of one source close to the negotiations earlier that month as to the likely release day for the Protocol.

Three weeks later, Emirates Team New Zealand issued a statement saying that they would not be competing in the 2014–15 Volvo Ocean Race, despite being linked to a Spanish sponsor. Entering the Volvo Ocean Race is a good fill-in option for the commercially sponsored America's Cup team. It provides visibility for the team and helps with cash flow from sponsors, and America's Cup sailors and others can be allocated to the Volvo entry. But it is a distraction.

Some damage may be inflicted on the team brand if the Volvo team doesn't perform — which often happens at some stage around

Emirates Team New Zealand placed a very creditable second with *Camper* behind *Groupama* in the 2011–12 Volvo Ocean Race. — RICHARD GLADWELL

the 40,000-nautical mile course. The Volvo is a race of many legs, and a loser one leg can be a winner the next.

All competitors won at least one leg in the previous race. The race does, of course, drain resources and take focus away from an America's Cup effort.

The statement, issued Friday, 2 May 2014, in Auckland, said:

'Emirates Team New Zealand announced today that it would not be competing in the next Volvo Ocean Race.

'In recent weeks, the team had explored a joint challenge with Spanish interests. The Volvo Ocean Race starts at Alicante, Spain, on October 4 this year.

'Grant Dalton said the team was not convinced it could mount a successful challenge in the time available and the team's energies would be better directed towards the next America's Cup.

'Dalton said the team had worked hard with excellent people representing the Spanish interests and with the Volvo Ocean Race management to get an entry to the start line.

'"In the end, time was against us. Every passing day magnified the impact that preparations for a round-the-world race would have on Emirates Team New Zealand's other operations.

'"The team exists to win the America's Cup. With the imminent announcement of the Protocol for the 35th America's Cup, it's time for us to withdraw reluctantly from any consideration of participation in the Volvo Ocean Race."'

The delay in announcing the Protocol, Class, venue and dates for the America's Cup was beginning to tell on the New Zealand team. They were asset rich with sheds full of kit, not knowing what should be kept and what should, or could, be sold as being surplus to requirements for the 35th America's Cup.

Lying in Hamble, UK, was *Camper*, the team's Volvo 70 which placed second in the last Volvo Ocean Race. She was listed for sale by the team at around NZ$1.5 million.

The potential Volvo partner deal was confirmed by both parties, with the Spanish group being led by Pedro Campos. His team had been sponsored by Spanish telco Telefónica, who had been a Volvo Ocean Race backer for the previous three editions.

Another Spanish company rumoured to be involved was MAPFRE, a Madrid-based insurance company that has been a long supporter of sailing but that started cutting back its sponsorships, including a long involvement in the then ISAF Sailing World Cup event at Palma. A third player was tipped to be El Corte Inglés, Europe's largest department-store chain.

The following day Emirates Team New Zealand CEO Grant Dalton said on Radio Live that the team was within 10 per cent of making the budget necessary to confirm the 2014–15 Volvo Ocean Race entry.

Dalton said they were 'very, very close. Normally we would take that financial risk, and historically we have bridged the gap. But it is not going to be easy to fund the America's Cup either.'

The team needed to conserve financial resources until the basic parameters of the next America's Cup became clear.

Earlier that day, Hamilton Island Yacht Club's Iain Murray confirmed that the key elements of the Protocol were agreed and that a signing process would be getting under way

as early as the next week. The Protocol was eventually signed and released four weeks later.

The AC62 Class Rule was also in circulation among the teams, but not yet officially published. The clear preference of the challengers was to return to San Francisco in the smaller, fully foiling catamaran.

The yachting correspondent of the UK's *The Independent* newspaper, the well-connected Stuart Alexander, had obtained details of the proposed class including the fact that a significant majority of the components would be one-design. But there was still nothing definite that could be put before a sponsor for sign-off.

Dalton said that Team New Zealand had a funding conflict between the Volvo Ocean Race campaign, quoted elsewhere as costing $17 million, and the America's Cup campaign which would cost around $70 million or so, provided challengers were restricted to a single boat, with a significant one-design element.

'We have two patients and only one lifejacket,' Dalton explained, 'and the team is about the America's Cup and the Volvo has to go by the wayside, unfortunately, but that is a commercial reality.

'We got 10 per cent away from meeting the budget,' he reiterated.

In the recent versions of the Volvo Ocean Race, the organisers work very closely with sponsors to provide full information on media coverage, and stopover promotional opportunities, so sponsors can be assured of a return on their investment, regardless of how their entry performs in the race.

'The [Volvo Ocean Race] organisation believed that the budget we had put together with them and the Spanish group we were working for was enough. But, honestly, we didn't believe that was correct and, in the end, just couldn't make it all work.

'Given a bit more time and taking a bit more risk, we probably could have made it work. But we have enough in to keep the America's Cup moving forward.'

Sail-World's sources at the time had it that the real reason for the Team New Zealand withdrawal was that the other parties felt that Dalton's budgets were too fat, and wanted him to reduce these further. Instead the New Zealand side of the entry equation walked

Iain Murray was Regatta Director for the 2017 America's Cup (top). Grant Dalton is interviewed by Peter Montgomery on 13 June 2014 (below). — RICHARD GLADWELL

away from that negotiation.

Dalton said the team was now focused on making their finances stretch until November when they expected the venue to be confirmed. 'I think it will roll pretty easily from there,' he added.

Dalton confirmed that the killer blow for the commercially driven Cup teams was precision on the venue, and the delay while the Defender, Golden Gate Yacht Club, played with five options — Chicago, San Diego, Hawaii and New York as well as San Francisco.

The new Protocol was publicly released on 2 June 2014, along with the AC62 Class Rule on 8 June 2014. (The next America's Cup would be sailed in a 62-ft wingsailed foiling catamaran, similar in many ways but 10 ft smaller than the class used in the 34th America's Cup in San Francisco.)

A few days later Oracle Team USA's Jimmy Spithill and Grant Dalton went head to head after media criticism of several aspects of the new Protocol.

Spithill hijacked a radio interview arranged to discuss San Francisco and its being eliminated as a Cup venue, but turned it around to make another attack on Team New Zealand and its CEO, saying 'that if the current management team of Team New Zealand isn't confident they can pull the team together or be competitive and win, then maybe the wrong people are running Team New Zealand.

'I could think of a couple of guys who could get in there and run it, who have a winning track record,' he added.

Spithill did not elaborate or name names, and the thrust of the remainder of the interview was that the newly announced Protocol was fair and that it would lower costs, due to the smaller boat and expected reduction in team size.

The six teams along with the new Commercial Commissioner are introduced at a media conference in St Pancras, London, September 2014. — GETTY

Spithill said that he expected the venue to be confirmed in October, ahead of the 31 December 2014 deadline set in the Protocol, which meant another seven months of conjecture and rumour.

A couple of days later, Team New Zealand's Chief Operating Officer, Kevin Shoebridge, weighed in during an interview with Newstalk ZB's Tony Veitch:

'To me it is bizarre. He [Spithill] has an unhealthy obsession with Team New Zealand, how it is managed, how it is funded and what its strategies are,' said Shoebridge. He went on to accuse Spithill of trash-talking the New Zealand team, and suggesting that Spithill's replacement management team for Team New Zealand were all close to Oracle Team USA.

Kevin Shoebridge, COO of Emirates Team New Zealand, is a Whitbread Round the World Race and America's Cup winner.

Public support was also fading fast, a big factor for New Zealand politicians with a general election coming up on 20 September 2014. An online poll conducted in a New Zealand newspaper showed that over 86 per cent of those responding believed that New Zealand should not challenge again for the America's Cup. Around 4500 people had responded to the poll, and only 14 per cent believed New Zealand should challenge again under the current Protocol.

That result made it tough for politicians to tip more investment into the team, with an election looming.

Grant Dalton, back from fundraising in Europe, did not respond directly to Spithill's comments. However, he would not have been surprised by them, as a concerted, and unsuccessful, campaign had been mounted some months previously to try to unseat the Team New Zealand management.

It was all just part of the America's Cup game — where the race can be won off the water as much as on. The event is not just a week-long match, but rather a three or four-year competition that starts the day after the previous match is concluded.

Winning the off-the-water battle was a big part of the Royal Perth Yacht Club's historic win with *Australia II* in 1983. It got the Kiwis out of the Louis Vuitton Cup in 1992, and of course played a big part in 2013.

At this stage whoever won the sledging war didn't really matter.

The fact was that, according to Dalton, the team was out of money in three weeks' time and his immediate task was to try to find funds to keep the team running until February 2015, when he expected to be generating sponsorship income. Part of the immediate target was to try to raise funds to pay for the US$2 million entry fee and US$1 million performance bond required by the new Protocol, which had to be lodged by the end of the year.

Dalton said that he had factored a US$1 million entry fee into his budgets, but had not expected to have to pony up with US$3 million (for entry fee and performance bond) by December 2014.

The first version of the Protocol was replaced within six days by a modified version after widespread criticism. In total, 16 articles in the first version were altered in the second edition.

Another 19 articles in the Protocol were amended and published on 13 October 2014. Although they did not reduce the US$3 million total of the entry fee and performance bond, they did slide the dates on which they would have to be paid in full by six months to 1 May 2015 — two years before the start of the America's Cup Regatta on 26 May 2017. Once paid, entry fees were non-refundable.

Dalton refuted Spithill's claims that the 35th America's Cup would be cheaper, saying that although the boat cost would be slightly cheaper, the campaign would be longer and more money would have to be spent on setting up a test platform ahead of the AC62 build.

Under the new Protocol, challengers were only allowed to build one boat, and the design-change options were more limited than in the previous Cup. The Defender could build two boats, as happened in the last Cup. (This created a furore among the general media, to which both Spithill and Coutts made the offer of the challengers being allowed to build a second AC62 — on the same time restrictions for use and conditions as the Defender.)

On the cost issue, Spithill fired back saying that 'anyone who says they can't run a campaign for less than last time is frankly being poorly managed, or giving themselves too big a pay rise'.

'The America's Cup isn't any cheaper, but in the end, it is the best event in the world for sailing, so we have got to be there,' was Dalton's closing response.

A week earlier when launching the Protocol for the 35th America's Cup, Oracle Team USA produced a promotional video which featured favourable comments from several challengers — Ben Ainslie Racing, Artemis Racing, Luna Rossa and the fledgling Team Australia, but not Team New Zealand.

Dalton's response was that the omission was a deliberate ploy by organisers. 'We're not going to blow smoke up Oracle's arse,' he retorted.

In response to claims that the latest Protocol was more commercial than those that had gone before, Dalton commented that there was nothing new in the Protocol in terms of commercial ideas, and that all had been tried before.

Responding to jibes from Spithill as to the amount Team New Zealand management and others were earning, Dalton put an 'educated guess' on Spithill's annual income from Oracle Team USA at US$3–5 million per year.

'Dean Barker earns a fraction of that,' Dalton added. He also revealed that of the office and management staff employed by Team New Zealand, only he and COO Kevin Shoebridge were on a full-time basis. There were others in the sailing, design and support teams who were on modest retainers. Dalton also revealed that wing trimmer Glenn Ashby had received a substantial offer from Team Australia to join the Challenger of Record.

Continuing with the theme that the Protocol was yet another attempt by Oracle Team USA to break up Team New Zealand, Dalton questioned why the Protocol had been loaded so heavily with US$3 million of performance bonds and entry fees, at that stage all payable before 31 December 2014 — well before even the America's Cup World Series gets under way, and for an America's Cup Match for which venues and dates had not yet been announced.

Dalton believed that was a move to strike at Team New Zealand's weakest point — being a lack of sponsorship income before 2015, and hitting at their ability to operate financially until that money came on stream. Dalton added that at this stage of the campaign Team New Zealand was in a better long-term position than it had ever been to secure sponsors for the next America's Cup.

'But I don't know whether we can even make it to next year,' he said.

The team had to survive financially until those sponsor commitments could be realised.

It was revealed on a Sunday morning television interview that Team New Zealand had already approached the New Zealand Government the previous Thursday looking for additional funding through its Trade and Enterprise arm. However, the Minister, Steven Joyce, said that was unlikely to be forthcoming. The team said they were looking to private sponsors and the marine industry to step up and see the team through the immediate period.

The team had already provided NZTE with a detailed business plan for the next America's Cup. Dalton commented that the team was also providing NZTE with very detailed budgets and payments made against those budgets, including individual salaries and other expenses, 'right down to the last paperclip'.

(Disclosure of how much Team New Zealand members are being paid is a favourite angle with talkback radio to get the lines and audiences fired up. In reality, however, publishing a list of salaries and remuneration would open up the team to poaching by wealthier teams. That happened in the 2000 and 2003 America's Cups where 35 New Zealanders sailed for other teams backed by billionaires and salaries sat in the US$30–40,000 range per month, for sailing crew.)

Time marched on, with the 30 June 2014 deadline fast approaching. The matter was one for the Board and team's Executive Committee.

As a separate exercise, the team was going through the Protocol in a very detailed way to determine whether it was so heavily stacked as to be unwinnable. Dalton said they would not enter if that were believed to be the situation, a comment which had been echoed in the Board's initial terms of reference.

Sailors are a superstitious lot. The number 13 is especially so. As for Black Friday — never start a voyage on one of those days. So, it seemed a little odd that Team New Zealand would call a media conference for Friday, 13 June 2014.

The state of play at that time was that the second version of the Protocol for the 35th America's Cup was just three days old. The view of the general media was that it was so skewed in favour of the Defender as to be unwinnable.

Emirates Team New Zealand had advanced proposals with a new sponsor, said to be a major bank. There had also been approaches made to private sponsors, along with the team's existing sponsor group.

The requirement for US$3 million in entry fees and performance bonds had come as a surprise to the team; it had been expected to be about US$1 million — given that under the Protocol for the 34th America's Cup in San Francisco, the same costs were initially closer to US$5 million and were later shaved to US$100,000. However, this time the entry fee went to a Regatta Officials Fund to cover the costs of running the completely independent America's Cup Regatta Management (ACRM).

Dalton opened the media session with a comment that most present probably expected a spray from him in the direction of Oracle Team USA's skipper, who had launched another media attack on the New Zealand team and its management on the previous day.

Generally, the Team New Zealand response was moderate and positive towards the Protocol, which was reported to have been labelled 'naked dictatorship' by the Italian America's Cup team.

Bermuda is announced as the venue for the 35th America's Cup at a media conference in New York City on 2 December 2014. — GETTY

After the media conference, the team issued a statement outlining six points of interest to the team in the Protocol — being the two-boats issue, the sidelining of the International Jury, timing of payment of entry fees, permission to sail in other (non-America's Cup events), the nationality rule, and the AC62 Class Rule (nine months later the AC62 was dropped and switched for the AC50 used in Bermuda).

In reality, there had been little change in the team's previously announced financial position — that the current cash lines would be exhausted by the end of June.

The team now had funding that would take them through to February 2015, 'but we need the Government to come in behind us and then we can make it [through to the end of the America's Cup]'.

The first question set the tone: 'How vital is the government funding?' to which Dalton responded that 'the government funding is absolutely vital. We have got more [money] than we said we would try and get, that has been pulled together since Thursday last week. Now the government funding is totally vital to our survival — or we are gone by the end of the month. We're not going to wait until the 30th of June to pull the plug on the place.'

Dalton added that he thought the government 'was very pro', that they were politically watching the mood of the country and the rhetoric around the Protocol and how that was playing out in the public domain.

After his opening comments, Dalton went completely off the cuff and made the point that in his experience, with two America's Cup campaigns under his belt, the team was in the best shape it had ever been with sponsors.

However, he realised he was in trouble and the media conference was starting to get out of control. Several times he turned to his two lieutenants COO Kevin Shoebridge and lawyer/rules advisor Russell Green to confirm points he had made, but it made him look unsure of his facts. But, government involvement aside, it was a good press conference with plenty of positives.

'We have a situation, given the right circumstances in terms of venues, we will fund the team. We can go forward,' he added. 'This time we have all sponsors, based on the criteria of knowing where it is, who would be prepared to go forward.

'Our immediate problem is to get to that point.'

They were also a 'mile further down the street' in terms of the technology in a foiling wingsailed multihull, compared to where they were at the start of the 2013 campaign, when few of them had even seen a wingsail and none had sailed catamarans.

Dalton thought the terms of the Protocol were quite workable — given that it was early days and there was process for changes to be made. The team also accepted the loss of San Francisco as a venue, but were happy with either San Diego or Chicago. Bermuda was not a preference for the team.

He was surprised to hear Oracle skipper Jimmy Spithill say that the challengers were offered a second AC62 but declined. When questioned whether the team would push for a second boat for each of the challengers, Dalton said that they were probably more interested in a training partnership with another challenger at the regatta or qualifier venue.

In terms of where Team New Zealand stood in regard to the US Defender, he noted that before embarking on the 2013 America's Cup programme none of the team had ever seen a wingsail, yet Oracle Team USA was embarking on its second wingsail multihulled campaign.

One of the criticisms of the team in the past campaign had been the belief that the management and Board of the team was a closed shop. In response to questioning on the relationship with the new Board, Dalton seemed to be very relaxed and confident that good progress was being made. The senior management of the team was meeting weekly with the Board. They also had an ongoing dialogue with the New Zealand Government. In fact, the only group they did not seem to be on speaking terms with was the Defender, Golden Gate Yacht Club, with whom Dalton said they had not had any direct communication. Discussions with the Challenger of Record had lapsed a few months previously.

The media conference ended around 4 pm. An hour later Dalton's 'ultimatum' to the government was put to Steven Joyce at an impromptu media conference in Wellington.

Joyce gave a limited rejection of a proposal by the team for further funding investment by New Zealand Trade and Enterprise, saying that there would be no more money from the government until team sponsors came to the party. But he did make the offer of some more immediate money from the government.

The Minister was clearly of the view that it should be possible for sponsors to inject money into the team, ahead of decisions by organisers on the America's Cup specifics, when these were broadly known.

'I think there is a limit to how far taxpayers should go and my preference is that they get some actual cash from their other commercial sponsors because this cannot be a government-

Steven Joyce, Minister of Finance in the National-led Government in 2017, made a conditional offer of initial funding in October 2013. — GETTY

funded challenge,' Joyce said.

The Minister made it clear in subsequent comments that he hadn't 'ruled out any cash injection. What I did say was that we put the $5 million in last October, which was getting them through to June. The expectation was that they would come up with some other funding in the meantime, and then that we would go forward.

'To be fair to them, they have had some trouble securing the information they need, but we feel at this point they should turn up with some sponsors' money as well as taxpayers' money.

'I have actually said, without going to my colleagues, that we would put in an extra couple of million, or so.'

Joyce told Newstalk ZB's Larry Williams that the team had initially come to him a couple of weeks previously looking for another $5 million, and were told 'to go away and try again'.

'Then Team New Zealand came back saying they actually need another $12 million and we've managed to find private individuals who would contribute five or six million, but they still needed another five million from the government.'

When asked where the sponsor commitment was coming from, the Minister said he had been told the sponsors were not prepared to commit without dates and venues.

'This cannot be a government-funded challenge,' Joyce repeated. 'But we can be part of it.'

The Minister said that there was an expectation that the taxpayer should be turning up on one basis, and the sponsors on another. The government's view seemed to be that they were being asked to contribute more, while the sponsors played for time and wouldn't get off their wallets.

'You're talking about well-known international brands,' said Joyce. 'In fact, worldwide brands, who know what the likely venues are going to be. I assume that Team New Zealand have been working hard with these people for seven months. What they need now is a contribution from the sponsors, not the whole sponsor investment. That is the way we have approached it with taxpayers. We've put in five and will put a little more in,' he added.

'For the life of me, I can't see why they can't get some sort of contribution from these big international sponsors,' Joyce said.

Two days later, the rift was still big news, pushing an All Blacks test win off the front page.

As the Protocol deadlines stood for the payment of entry fees and the performance bond, Team New Zealand required $5 million to see them through to the end of December and an additional $6 million to get to the end of February 2015.

Dalton revealed he had found commercial and private commitments, including from new investors, for $6 million of that $11 million total — an impressive achievement in the seven days.

'In a week we have found six million dollars of funding ourselves, that is absolutely correct,' Dalton told the *Sunday Star-Times*.

With the Team New Zealand Board due to meet on the Monday, Sir Stephen Tindall flew back into the country that morning to continue discussions on how the syndicate could finish

---

Water spray over ETNZ's cyclors graphically shows the streamlined profile presented by the team and how this fits perfectly with the aerodynamics of the overall design package. — Richard Gladwell

tackling its potentially terminal financial situation — still facing a deadline of just 14 days before their money ran out. The following Saturday, Tindall told Newstalk ZB that the team had the funds for another six months, without further government support.

'We were facing closure a week ago,' said Tindall. 'But some of us have put our hands in our pockets, and we now have enough money to get us through to the end of the year. We are more confident every day that we are going to be able to challenge, and we will worry about government funding later on.'

Responding to questions regarding Dalton's long-term role with the team, Tindall responded: 'He [Dalton] is a master at raising the money.

Sir Stephen Tindall has supported Emirates Team New Zealand since 1995 and has been a Board member and chairman since May 2015.

— RICHARD GLADWELL

The sponsors all know him very well; he has got private guys that help. I think that if Grant went, we're dead.

'We've just got to stay the course, stay resolute as a board, and we'll get ourselves through this.'

Tindall described the current phase of the America's Cup as the 'Valley of Death', and something that occurs every Cup cycle for the team that relies heavily on commercial sponsorship.

'We're fighting for our lives to get through, but this always happens,' Tindall told Newstalk ZB host Tony Veitch. 'Back in the year 2000, I got a phone call from a trustee straight after we had re-won the America's Cup, and was told we're completely out of money, and if we don't raise some money tonight we're going to lose Russell Coutts and Brad Butterworth. We need $8 million tonight.'

In response, Tindall said he would put up

$4 million immediately if someone else put up the rest.

'We had a handshake agreement with those two, and ten days later they went to Alinghi.'

Tindall added that it was the same for all commercial teams, who had to retain their talent immediately after the conclusion of an America's Cup, or another team would snaffle up the talent.

Former Team New Zealand tactician Brad Butterworth confirmed that he had offered to assist the team in whatever way he could. But Tindall's response to that was that Butterworth would only be involved if he were CEO, and the Board was not inclined to accept his offer.

Later in the week, four-time America's Cup winner Brad Butterworth appeared in a prime-time news show interview in New Zealand to explain why he wanted to rejoin Team New Zealand. Butterworth believed that Team New Zealand needed a shake-up, starting at the top.

'It's not about me. I just thought that I could help,' said Butterworth. 'That's what I've said to the new Board, that I have made myself available if they want to talk to me or if they wanted to consider changing people at the top of the tree.

'Dalton said himself before the last Cup, that if he didn't win it this time then he was out and that he should let someone else have a go,' said Butterworth. 'Really it's a matter of me saying that there are a lot of people that I know in the Cup that say that I should get in there and try and help them.'

Three and a half months later, the urgent financial pressure on cash flow reduced when the Protocol was amended to allow the deferred payment in instalments of the entry fee, and the deferral of payment of the performance bond by a further four months to 1 May 2015. In a further amendment in April 2015, the payment terms were stretched even further, allowing the performance bond to be paid in instalments, with the final instalment being due in October 2015. That effectively gave teams a further 10 months for payment.

But the sting in the tail of this piece of generosity was that the teams who paid on the extended schedule lost their voting rights on the Competitor Forum and Challenger Committee from 1 May 2015 until they became fully paid.

The fallout from Black Friday shook the team to its core and tainted the relationship with the government and its fans right up to the start of the America's Cup Regatta.

The media-driven saga took the eventual winner of the America's Cup to the brink of closure two years before the start of the 35th Match in Bermuda. It was all triggered by less than a minute of a 40-minute media conference.

Team New Zealand never held that style of media conference again, which had served them well right back into Blake's day. The next attempt at getting information out into the public domain was an awkward video where Dalton and Kevin Shoebridge answered set-piece questions on camera from a PR journalist. Thereafter communication was by media release, email or the occasional interview where they had some control over what was being reported.

The attacks and sledging on Team New Zealand continued right through to the America's Cup, with the #letsgetdalton social media sideshow in May 2015, and with the team responding by self-styling themselves as the 'Lone Wolf' right through the America's Cup cycle.

Chapter 5

The Lone Wolf starts to prowl

The last three America's Cups have all had one thing in common — the initial Challenger of Record has resigned, or been ruled invalid, early in the cycle.

The result has been a poorly thought-out Protocol, initially stacked in favour of the Defender and one which triggers acrimony from the day it is first announced and continues for the duration of that America's Cup cycle.

The 35th America's Cup followed a familiar pattern. Around 19 July 2014 the Challenger of Record, Hamilton Island Yacht Club, advised that they would be withdrawing from the 35th America's Cup. The move followed a competitor meeting called by them in Los Angeles the previous weekend.

A similar situation occurred in the 34th America's Cup, when Golden Gate Yacht Club accepted a challenge from Club Nautico di Roma

(Mascalzone Latino) on very favourable terms to the Defender. That club also pulled out, saying they could not find the financial sponsorship to continue, after negotiating the Protocol.

In the 33rd America's Cup, Golden Gate Yacht Club called out Club Nautíco Español de Vela (CNEV), the club whose Letter of Challenge was accepted by Société Nautique de Genève (SNG), the Swiss club of 2003 and 2007 America's Cup champion Alinghi.

The Spanish club admitted during a hearing that they were a 'legal adjustment' and had been in place for just two weeks, after the Spanish national sailing authority (RFEV) had planned to be the Challenger. But on a re-read of the Deed of Gift, lawyers for the Spanish national authority realised that they were not a body that was entitled to challenge and so quickly incorporated a new yacht club, CNEV, with five of the directors of RFEV as its only declared members.

The ensuing legal shambles took three years to resolve through the New York State legal

---

The 2013 America's Cup was sailed on San Francisco Bay home waters of the Golden Gate Yacht Club. — RICHARD GLADWELL

system, and shrank the challengers from 11 in the 2007 Louis Vuitton Cup to just three in the 2013 event.

Announcing their decision to withdraw as the Challenger of Record, the Hamilton Island Yacht Club said: 'The Challenge was initiated with a view to negotiating a format for the 35th America's Cup that was affordable and put the emphasis back on sailing skills.

'Ultimately our estimate of the costs of competing were well beyond our initial expectation and our ability to make the formula of our investment and other commercial support add up.'

Hamilton Island Yacht Club CEO Iain Murray said that the decision to withdraw or not enter the 35th America's Cup was only made in the 48 hours before it was announced — about two weeks before entry deadline.

'We've had a detailed assessment of the campaign, and have had expert advice from a lot of companies that deal in the commercial area. Even though I think the commercial feeling is very positive towards the America's Cup, the timeline is the killer in this Cup.

'Sponsors want to know where the venues are, and the dates. The gap gets pretty wide trying to get the sponsors to commit against the timeline of the expenditure.'

Under the Deed of Gift, the 19th-century

Superyachts moored along Front Street at Hamilton, Bermuda. The British Overseas Territory hosted the 35th America's Cup. — RICHARD GLADWELL

document that governs the ongoing conduct of the America's Cup, the first Challenger to file a Letter of Challenge with the Defender becomes what is known as the Challenger of Record. That yacht club then undertakes the process of sorting out the terms of the Match with the defending club, in this case the Golden Gate Yacht Club of San Francisco.

Those terms are known as the Protocol, which runs until the America's Cup Match has been sailed, when the process starts again. The Protocol contains the provision for there to be more than one Challenger accepted, and they sail off in a Challenger Selection Series better known as the Louis Vuitton Cup.

The whole of the challenging process is carefully arranged so that a friendly challenge is accepted, under prearranged circumstances.

Hamilton Island YC's challenge was made by a business representative of the Oatley's wine company as the 19th race in the 2013 America's Cup was finishing. A second, backup challenge was believed to have been filed at the time.

The club's proposed challenge was with a 90-ft monohull for a match to be sailed in early September 2017. (Some aspects of the Match can be varied by mutual consent between the challenging and defending clubs in the Protocol.)

The contemporary practice has been for the Challenger to name a boat which complies with

Bermuda's Great Sound is dotted with limestone mansions, some dating back to the 17th century.

— RICHARD GLADWELL

the terms of the Deed of Gift, and then the two parties negotiate a suitable class, which was the AC62 — a 62-ft wingsailed catamaran, a shorter and more refined version of the AC72 used in the 34th America's Cup.

If the Challenger of Record drops out, the mantle falls to the next challenge received. Overall there is little effect, at this stage, other than the number of challengers reduces by one. During the Match, as one Challenger of Record is eliminated, they are replaced by the next-entered team who is still alive in the regatta.

The primary advantage of the Challenger of Record role is the ability to negotiate a Protocol and to have the power of approval [veto] on any changes. The initial Challenger of Record has never won the America's Cup, and the role is widely regarded as being a poisoned chalice.

The Protocol for the 35th Match was announced on 2 June 2014, eight months after the conclusion of the previous Match. During the negotiation, there were significant points of disagreement between then Challenger and Defender over the split venues, the media rights, and costs. Those issues still remained along with a lack of oversight by the then International Sailing Federation, the world controlling body for sailing (now known as World Sailing).

Murray said the decision to not proceed further in the 35th America's Cup Regatta was made only after the Competitors Meeting held in Los Angeles in July 2014. That meeting was called by Hamilton Island Yacht Club, not by the Defender.

'The Competitors Meeting was the last stage in a world trip,' he said. 'We were initially focused on commercial opportunities. When we arrived back in Australia, we reported on that exercise and the Competitors Meeting. The Board took the position they have just announced.'

Murray would not be drawn on his working relationship with Russell Coutts, CEO of the America's Cup Event Authority (ACEA). 'I spoke to him yesterday for the first time in three months,' Murray said. 'I am sure Russell is disappointed we've withdrawn. We have spoken to most of the teams, and they are all disappointed.

'We have given 90 days' notice of our intention to withdraw as we are required to do under the Protocol,' said Murray.

Luna Rossa, through their club Circolo della Vela Sicilia (CVS), as the next club to have lodged a Letter of Challenge, took over the role of Challenger of Record. Under the terms of the Protocol, they, along with the Defender, had the right of approval (effectively a veto) on any changes proposed to be made to the Protocol.

Nine months later in March 2015, the Italian Challenger elected to turn that right over to the majority vote of the Challenger Committee, which at that stage consisted of the teams of five challenging clubs.

Luna Rossa has always been very popular in New Zealand since they first entered the America's Cup in 2000 and were the Challenger in the 31st Match against the Russell Coutts-skippered Team New Zealand. Francesco de Angelis, their skipper in 2000 and 2003 in Auckland and again in 2007 in Valencia, was made an Honorary Officer of the New Zealand Order of Merit (ONZM). At the time, de Angelis was voted the second-sexiest man in New Zealand.

The patron of Luna Rossa, Patrizio Bertelli, along with his wife Miuccia Prada, is the co-chief executive officer of the Prada Group, a top international luxury goods manufacturer and retailer.

On most issues in the conduct of the America's Cup — not just in the 2017 series, but in previous editions — the New Zealand and Italian teams would usually vote along the same lines on changes to the Protocol under which the America's Cup Regatta is conducted and also the class rules which govern the yacht that is used. A degree of control over changes could be exercised, even though Luna Rossa and Team New Zealand would be in the minority on some Protocol changes, because of the right of approval on changes possessed by the Challenger of Record.

For the 35th America's Cup, the Italian team was the first to get properly established,

hiring 80 staff and establishing a full America's Cup base in Cagliari, on the southern coast of Sardinia, Italy. The team had also converted two AC45s to become fully foiling as a staging point for the AC62 — the then America's Cup Class.

On 13 October 2014, the challengers agreed that the Challenger of Record's rights would be handed over to the Challenger Committee and be exercised by a majority vote of that committee. The magnanimous gesture was a huge mistake and one which saw Luna Rossa exit the Cup, on a point of principle, less than six months later. It is unclear whether Luna Rossa had read the Challenger Committee tea

Bermuda was formed by two volcanic calderas. The Great Sound is on the left with the Royal Naval Dockyard at the far tip of the Sound. — SCOTT STALLARD

leaves at the time they agreed to hand over their right of veto on Protocol changes. It was set to end in tears — just a matter of when.

Only one Protocol change was passed on 10 December 2014, relating to an adjustment of team numbers allowed to attend an America's Cup World Series regatta — a very minor change in the grand scheme of the 35th America's Cup.

The spotlight shifted over the next few months to the vexed issue of venue selection, after the announcement was made on 9 July 2014 that Chicago had been given a 'Dear

John' letter saying that they were no longer in consideration for the Match venue, but would be an option for a World Series event.

That left the options of San Diego and Bermuda still on the table. The challengers had previously expressed a preference to return to San Francisco when there were four options available.

Under the Deed of Gift, the right to select a venue lies with the Defender. Many scholars of the America's Cup say that the implied intention of the donors of the 19th-century trophy was that it should be contested on the home waters of the defending club. That would have meant that Golden Gate YC would have no option but to defend on San Francisco Bay. But none of

---

Team Australia was the team of Challenger of Record, Hamilton Island Yacht Club and sailed initially in Sydney with Oracle Team USA. — ANDREA FRANCOLINI

the challenging clubs were too keen to take that one back into the New York Supreme Court for a ruling.

The Deed of Gift does specify that the regatta must be sailed under the rules of the defending club, unless they were modified under the mutual consent provisions of the Deed of Gift.

(The then International Yacht Racing Union was only beginning to be formed in 1907 — over 55 years after the schooner *America* contested a race around the Isle of Wight for the £100 Cup, the Victorian ewer which became known as the America's Cup named after the winner, not the first nation to hold it.)

Many quite incorrectly believe that because of the Mutual Consent provision the winner of the America's Cup has the right to dictate the basics of the next event. Under the Deed of Gift, a superbly drafted document, the America's Cup is a challenge trophy — meaning it is Challenger-driven not Defender-led. The Challenger names the boat and its dimensions, and the dates for the Challenge, which must be named at least 10 months in advance.

The only conditions of the regatta which can be altered by the Mutual Consent provisions of the Deed relate to the conditions under which the racing may be conducted. There cannot be an alteration of the basic tenets of the Deed of Gift — specifically the maximum and minimum length of the yacht, and that they have to be powered by sails alone, and constructed in the country of the Challenger and Defender clubs.

If this were not the case, the Cup could be contested in 30-ft production powerboats sourced from a foreign builder.

It is believed that the 2017 America's Cup Challenger, Sweden's Artemis Racing, were originally planning to build their Challenger at their San Francisco base. But when Team New Zealand raised issues about compliance with the Constructed in Country provisions of the Deed of Gift, Artemis Racing switched the build of their yacht to Sweden and averted any subsequent legal complaints had they won the Cup.

The concept of hawking the venue for the America's Cup is a recent one and began with the defence by Alinghi in 2007, when they elected not to sail the Match on their home waters (Lake Geneva) and instead worked with options including Cascais, Portugal and Valencia, Spain. The latter got the nod by Alinghi principal Ernesto Bertarelli, reportedly against the wishes of his skipper, Russell Coutts, causing a serious rift between the two, and Coutts was replaced as Alinghi skipper by Ed Baird (USA) for the 2007 America's Cup Defence.

The 2017 venue selection process was viewed askance by the challengers, particularly when their preferred option, the home waters of the Golden Gate Yacht Club on San Francisco Bay, was the first to be dropped.

The bidding details were kept confidential, but when it got down to the final decision it was a trade-off between a solid deal from Bermuda involving a US$15 million event fee paid in four instalments, a US$25 million underwrite of any event sponsorship shortfall, and the US$37 million spend on development of infrastructure at the Royal Naval Dockyard at the entrance to the Great Sound, venue for the racing. (The Bermudian dollar is pegged to the US dollar 1:1.)

Of that expenditure, it was possible that only the event fee would go to the regatta organisers. Bermuda was projecting a US$250 million return on their investment, plus a tax take of

US$14 million. (Infrastructure costs are not normally attributed to an event as a cost, as they relate to building a permanent facility and ongoing legacy or white elephant to the host region.)

San Diego, by contrast, is reported to have offered 10,000 free bed nights to accommodate people associated with the America's Cup. The area for the Match was to be on the largely landlocked inner San Diego Bay.

Although not stated publicly, it is believed that part of the original deal with Hamilton Island Yacht Club would be that the Qualifier Series of the America's Cup Regatta would be sailed in the southern hemisphere, probably at an Australian venue during the summer (December–March). Then the top four challengers, plus the Defender, would be shipped to Bermuda ready for the Playoffs (Semi-Finals) and Finals and the 35th America's Cup Match itself.

Under that arrangement, the regatta would be relatively long-running (spread over five or six months), which gives added exposure to team sponsors, and would take in the summer months in two hemispheres. It was a concept which had a lot of merit.

There was also the possibility of a further event fee and other commercially favourable terms for the America's Cup organisers and maybe challengers.

Golden Gate Yacht Club was the Defender for the 2013 and 2017 America's Cups, but only defended once in its home waters. — RICHARD GLADWELL

The two downsides were that only four challengers would sail in Bermuda. There was also increased cost from having to set up bases in two locations and freight from Europe or Bermuda, where several of the teams had already become established.

A couple of weeks after the Challengers Meeting in Los Angeles called by the then Challenger of Record, Hamilton Island Yacht Club, a second meeting was held in London at the behest of the event organisers, the America's Cup Event Authority.

Five teams attended — being the three entered teams: Artemis Racing (Sweden), Luna Rossa (Italy), Land Rover BAR (UK), plus the fledgling Team France along with Defender Oracle Team USA.

The reasons for New Zealand being 'dis-invited' were not disclosed but were believed to have been triggered by the team's refusal to sign a statement endorsing all venues including Bermuda. Writing in *The Independent*, Stuart Alexander described it this way:

'Missing will be Kevin Shoebridge, who represented TNZ at a Challenger meeting in Los Angeles called by the then lead Challenger, Australia's Hamilton Island Yacht Club, which a few days later announced its intention to withdraw from the next cup in 2017.

'TNZ spoke to Russell Coutts last week and at that time expected to be at the London meeting

Emirates Team New Zealand's Grant Dalton with Luna Rossa's Max Sirena who was assigned to the New Zealand team for the 35th America's Cup. — RICHARD GLADWELL

but was then told no. "We were disinvited," said a senior observer. None of the others wanted to comment on the Kiwi exclusion. A spokesman for the America's Cup Event Authority, also run by Coutts, said: "I can't help you."

'The agenda for the London meeting is being kept confidential but is not thought to include persistent offers from the San Francisco Bay city of Alameda to host the teams, all of which have said they would be willing to contribute in any way possible to keep the event in SFO.

'ACEA says only San Diego and Bermuda are still in the running. But the teams have only just over a week to lodge formal challenges and the first tranche of US$1 million entry fee. The entry deadline is midnight PST in SFO on 8 August. The venue and even some format decisions will be weeks after that.'

For Emirates Team New Zealand, it would have been commercial suicide for the Kiwis to sign such a statement, as they were well aware that the New Zealand Government was interested in backing the team for a USA or European location, but there was no appetite for the Atlantic archipelago of Bermuda.

The reason for two meetings in two weeks, when none had been held for the previous 10 months, is a little hard to understand.

Two weeks earlier Stuart Alexander in *The Independent* outlined the position of the first Challengers Meeting held in Los Angeles as follows:

'The six from the UK, Australia, New Zealand, France, Italy and Sweden took the opportunity to say that they disapproved of the move to drop San Francisco as the venue, expressed varying degrees of dislike for the two remaining venue choices, San Diego and Bermuda, made clear that they did not want the event split between two venues, one possibly in the southern hemisphere, and wanted to see supervisory provisions, which at the moment bypass the sport's world governing body, the Southampton-based International Sailing Federation (ISAF), reviewed.'

Alexander's report of the meeting (no report was published) was confirmed as being substantially correct by Iain Murray of Hamilton Island Yacht Club, who at that stage was still in negotiations with Golden Gate Yacht Club and their marketing and event management arm, America's Cup Event Authority.

Two weeks later the tune had changed completely.

The official media release from London said in part that the meeting was positive, and six points were agreed of which three were curiously interesting in the light of what was to come. First, all the teams present agreed that they would commit — if they were to win the Cup in 2017 — to continue with the America's Cup World Series. Second, a commitment was made to further reduce the costs for both this Cup and future editions. Third, support for the choice of host venue, be it Bermuda or San Diego. Fourth, commitment to a working group to agree on the date and event structure of the 36th America's Cup, to lay the foundations for a sustainable event.

Points 1 and 4 were setting the scene for what became known as 'The Framework', a mildly controversial, secret agreement relating to the ongoing conduct of the America's Cup,

---

AC50s under construction at Core Builders Composites' facility (top) in Warkworth, north of Auckland and Southern Spars (bottom), West Auckland.

announced in a meeting to which Emirates Team New Zealand was again not invited or did not attend (depending on who is to be believed), held again in London, over two years later in November 2016.

Where two weeks previously the teams had expressed 'varying degrees of dislike' for the two remaining venues Bermuda and San Diego, they now supported the choice of either. The decider for Emirates Team New Zealand was that the teams did not support a split venue for the America's Cup Challenger Selection Series.

From that juncture matters played out as signalled. Hamilton Island Yacht Club withdrew as Challenger of Record on 19 July 2014. Luna Rossa, or rather their club Circolo della Vela Sicilia, took over that role and later handed their rights as Challenger of Record to the newly formed Challenger Committee — where decisions were made by a majority vote.

Next, Brigadier General Dr Harvey Schiller was appointed as Commercial Commissioner for the America's Cup on 29 August 2014 — working in the America's Cup Event Authority. The former pilot and decorated Vietnam veteran had a background in sports management, Turner Sports, and the US Olympic Committee.

Iain Murray, former Regatta Director for the 34th America's Cup, then head of new Challenger of Record Team Australia and part of the negotiating team for the Protocol for the 35th America's Cup, was again appointed Regatta Director for the 35th America's Cup.

Finally, Bermuda was announced as the venue on 3 December 2014.

Grant Dalton said they had knowledge of the venue and that the announcement was 'not a bombshell' for the team.

The announcement of Bermuda as the venue was made at a media conference in Manhattan, New York attended by General Schiller and Bermuda Premier Michael Dunkley. Schiller confirmed receipt of 'a serious proposal from Team New Zealand to stage a major event'.

The event was clearly the America's Cup Qualifier Series, which was planned for the southern hemisphere and which had dropped into Emirates Team New Zealand's lap with the withdrawal of Hamilton Island Yacht Club. However, the way was also open for other southern hemisphere cities to bid for the event.

The Qualifier Series venue was to be determined by America's Cup Event Authority. Under the Protocol the series could last no more than 30 days, and had to commence no earlier than four months prior to the America's Cup Playoffs (Semi-Finals and Finals for the Challenger Selection Series), to be sailed in Bermuda. The Playoffs were required to be started 25 days before, and conclude three days before the Match.

If the southern hemisphere Qualifier Series went ahead, all teams would set up in Auckland several months in advance and train from the Viaduct area. Based on previous America's Cup events, the Qualifier would have significant economic impact.

Auckland had the advantage of twice being a previous America's Cup venue and has substantial marine industry infrastructure. Oracle Team USA also had their construction facility based in Warkworth — an hour's drive north of Auckland. Southern Spars, who built Emirates Team New Zealand's AC50, are located in West Auckland. North Sails and Doyle Sails have major facilities in Auckland.

The build-up period to the Qualifiers would be vital to the teams, giving them ready access to good boat-construction facilities if there was damage or substantial modifications required to the AC62s.

The event was also expected to attract substantial media coverage, both in the build-up and in the Qualifier itself — which is the equivalent of the round-robin series of the former Louis Vuitton Cup. It was also set to be the first and only time that the challengers would come up against the Defender in an indicator series ahead of the 35th Match.

Turning back to the government involvement, or rather a decision not to be involved because of the Bermuda venue, Dalton was upbeat. 'At this stage we will be there, I can tell you that, but it is a day-to-day moving target. Bermuda is new, not to us because we have known about it for two weeks.

'It is my job to ensure that 29 years of involvement in the America's Cup by Team New Zealand continues.'

The events of the next three months would put that last statement to a severe test, but already the Lone Wolf was prowling.

The front element of a wingsail under construction at Core Builders Composites, who built components for several teams. — RICHARD GLADWELL

Chapter 6

Enter Burling and Tuke

Dean Barker copped plenty of flak for not winning the America's Cup in San Francisco. The non-sailing media were the most vociferous, but the sailing-savvy media took a more measured view.

With the points score at 8–1, in New Zealand's favour in the best of 19 race series, Barker and his team took a ragging from his opposite number, Jimmy Spithill. In this regard, Spithill was ably assisted by many elements of the New Zealand media who, as in the 2003 defence debacle, always looked for a scapegoat — a single point of responsibility who could be summarily executed, before moving on to solving the next sporting crisis.

One instance was the media conference called for 5 May 2003, to reveal the contents of a review into Team New Zealand's sorry defence performance. The session at the Royal New

Zealand Yacht Squadron was heavily attended by some sailing media, but mostly general and sports media. It was a lynch mob.

Team New Zealand Director Peter Menzies fronted the media. The Auckland businessman was one of three directors appointed by Russell Coutts and Brad Butterworth before they left the team after the successful 2000 defence.

After giving an overview of the report, Menzies took questions. One of the first was: 'Who is going to be held accountable?'

Menzies gave the reply that it was a complex situation and there was no single person or issue that could be blamed.

Not satisfied with that response, the reporter put her head down and had another charge. 'Can you tell us who was responsible?'

Again, Menzies answered that it involved the whole team, multiple factors and not just a single individual.

Used to dealing with politicians who wouldn't answer a question directly, the frustrated senior news reporter put her point directly: 'When are

---

Peter Burling (left) and Blair Tuke, Gold medallists in the 49er skiff class at the 2016 Rio Olympics. — RICHARD GLADWELL heads going to roll?'

Menzies deftly gave a different version of the same answer to her previous two questions and moved on.

Some did leave the team after the 2003 America's Cup. But they did it quietly, with their heads still attached to their bodies, and either joined another sailing team or got a 'real job', without becoming click-bait.

That same scenario was often played out in the 14 years that led to the win in Bermuda.

It got to the point, after the Black Friday media conference on 13 June 2014, that the team stopped holding media conferences where senior team members would face a media battery — often just looking to spill blood over a misjudged sentence.

Dean Barker had been with Team New Zealand since the 1995 campaign when he had a five-month involvement, turning down an invitation to go to San Diego. Instead he chose to return to his own campaign to represent New Zealand in the 1996 Olympics in the Finn class. He finished second in the selection trials, off Gulf Harbour, losing the Olympic nomination on the final day to 1992 Olympic Bronze medallist Craig Monk who had sailed as a grinder in the 1995 America's Cup.

Monk stepped back into the Finn for a late run at the Olympics in the heavyweight men's singlehander in which Barker had put in the hard yards to achieve a very creditable world ranking of fifth, and was the favourite for selection. Monk went on to finish in 13th at Savannah.

For the 2000 defence, Barker helmed *NZL-57*, the 'mushroom boat' or trial-horse, against Russell Coutts. He scored his first America's Cup race win in the final race of the 2000 America's Cup, sharing the America's Cup presentation with Coutts. Barker was aged just 26 years old — the same age as Peter Burling in the Bermuda win.

With Coutts and the tight five shifting to Alinghi for the 2003 America's Cup, Barker, just turned 27, stepped into the skipper's role.

Most will remember Barker for having finished second in three successive America's Cups — in an event where there is no second.

On the credit side of Barker's ledger, after the 2013 America's Cup, he had won 11 races in America's Cup racing, the same as his rival Jimmy Spithill (excluding the 2010 Deed of Gift Match which was a closed event and not open to other challengers). Barker's wins were scored across three America's Cups, Spithill's across one, or two — again excluding the closed Deed of Gift Match.

But in the eyes of the general sporting media, Barker was portrayed as a has-been and a choker. In reality, his America's Cup record was up there with the other top three helmsmen of the modern era — Coutts, Conner and Spithill.

When Emirates Team New Zealand arrived home from San Francisco, there were obviously going to have to be some hard calls made on a number of areas and people.

The shift from an open design boat to the one-design hulls, some components and a one-design profile wingsail meant that the composition of the design team would have to change — with specialists being needed to focus on the areas of design that still had a freedom of choice.

These moves were made in the interests of cost reduction — to shrink the size of design teams — and to stop teams spending enormous amounts of money and effort in pursuing design angles that would yield only a small speed gain.

For instance, in the AC72, with unrestricted wingsail shape, many hours had been spent by the teams on finding the ultimate shape. Yet when notes were compared after the 2013 America's Cup, the difference was only about 3 per cent between the shapes — so going to a one-design profile shape made a lot of sense.

Also, if the top teams grabbed most of the design talent, there were slim pickings left for the start-up teams. That in turn lowered entry numbers in an event which had to grow substantially to regain its credibility. It was a sound move to reduce the design scope in the new class.

One of the criticisms of Team New Zealand was that it was a closed shop, that it wasn't really a New Zealand team, just a bunch of Kiwi sailors whose faces fitted with the current hierarchy. That it was salary first and performance second.

The reality is that it is extremely hard to run any meaningful trial in America's Cup boats. There are too many nuances. There was no template for the perfect skipper or helmsman. Sure, you could put the grinders through some form of fitness and strength tests. But how do you measure the crew chemistry on the boat — so they all worked in the same direction without any schisms when they were losing a race and needed to turn things around quickly on the water?

The shift to one-design America's Cup boats

Emirates Team New Zealand skipper Dean Barker (right) in full kit in San Francisco, with tactician Ray Davies alongside. — RICHARD GLADWELL

and to a slightly lesser extent with the surrogate boats or test boats opened up the options for some real crew selection in a similar way to how seat racing is run in rowing.

With a crew of just five or six, two sailing teams, and a couple of one-design boats, it is possible to switch crew between boats, one at a time, until the fastest combination is found.

A month after Grant Dalton had returned from a two-and-a-half-month stint in Europe going around sponsors and backers and recruiting, Team New Zealand called a media conference on 14 January 2014, to announce that they had signed up 2012 Olympic Silver medallists Blair Tuke and Peter Burling, who were also the current world champions in the 49er skiff.

That move gave the team the option of pitching one experienced crew of Barker and tactician Ray Davies against a second young crew led by Burling and Tuke who had won the Red Bull Youth America's Cup sailed in AC45s ahead of the 2013 America's Cup in San Francisco.

Emirates Team New Zealand had an embarrassment of riches — particularly compared to some of the other top teams who lacked the sufficient local talent to be able to put together a national team and instead opted to recruit the best team of professional sailors that money could buy.

Finance permitting, the programme was to sail two AC45s in the America's Cup World Series, with Barker/Davies on one boat and Burling/Tuke in the other — introducing a level of competitive selection that has long been lacking in the team.

Even if Burling and Tuke had prevailed in that selection process, Barker could have still retained a role as Sailing Director. However, it subsequently emerged that the role had been allocated to Glenn Ashby, who was also skipper and wingsail trimmer in the eventual America's Cup crew.

Three months later, with none of the basic questions about the 35th America's Cup answered by organisers, the financial siege of Team New Zealand continued and began to take its toll. The prospect of Team New Zealand having the luxury of running multiple test boats with two crews competing faded fast as the team had to start

Peter Burling (17 years) sailed in his first Olympics at Qingdao, 2008, and with Blair Tuke in Weymouth (2012) and in Rio (2016). — RICHARD GLADWELL

conserving financial resources just to survive.

The new Board had come on stream in early April 2014 and was charged to determine whether another challenge was viable. That triggered a formal review of team performance and what was required to win — at the yet to be announced venue, in the yet to be announced class, on the yet to be announced dates.

Team decision making was also in the hands of a six-person Executive Committee, of which Dean Barker, as skipper and Sailing Director, was a member. (Many confuse the position of skipper as being another name for the helmsman. On some teams, the two are one and the same. On Emirates Team New Zealand in 2017 Glenn Ashby, for various reasons including having the most multihull sailing experience, was both sail trimmer as well as leading the crew as skipper. Peter Burling had the single task of helmsman. In the 2013 America's Cup Dean Barker had the dual role of helmsman and skipper. It is a significant difference.)

In that review, it was decided to replace Barker as skipper. However, the news did not break until nine months later in February 2015. It is hard to believe that, as an Executive Committee member, Barker was unaware that the decision had been taken to replace him in that role; however, that is Barker's view of the situation.

In the meantime, internationally sourced rumours swirled with the New Zealand skipper

Emirates Team New Zealand skipper and Sailing Director Glenn Ashby is one of the world's most accomplished multihull sailors. — GETTY

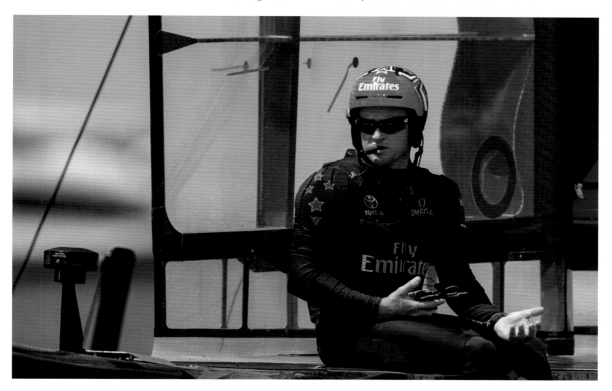

After leaving Emirates Team New Zealand, Dean Barker moved to new team SoftBank Team Japan as CEO, skipper and helmsman. — RICHARD GLADWELL

being linked to Luna Rossa and that one of the Italians' helmsmen was to be exited to make way for the New Zealander. Rumours of Barker joining Luna Rossa, though, had surfaced previously and had amounted to nothing.

There were also international whisperings that if Team New Zealand collapsed, their key people would be snapped up by an Asian entry which was waiting in the wings.

Later, on 8 May 2015, SoftBank Team Japan had their challenge accepted by Golden Gate Yacht Club with the team being partnered with Oracle Team USA, whose CEO was Russell

Coutts, Barker's former skipper in the 2000 America's Cup Defence. Dean Barker was announced as the Japanese skipper two weeks later.

Barker's ousting was first broken on social media, which Team New Zealand claimed and still maintain was as much a surprise to them as it was to Barker.

To the experienced sailing media, the news was no surprise. The scene had been set over a year ago in January 2014 when Burling and Tuke were announced to a media conference at the old Alinghi, now Team New Zealand, base in Halsey Street.

In February 2014, the sailing programme got under way with four sailors from Team New Zealand competing at the International A-class catamaran Worlds at Takapuna. They ran a programme of sorts out of the Halsey Street base. Glenn Ashby was at that stage a seven-time world champion in the 18-ft singlehander, on which the helmsman sails from a trapeze. To further complicate matters, foiling had just been introduced to the class. Ashby won his eighth world title at Takapuna. Tuke, no slouch as a helmsman, beat Burling to finish second. Tactician Ray Davies finished fifth. Dean Barker watched from a team RIB.

A similar mini-campaign was enacted for the foiling Moth Worlds held in early January 2015 in Sorrento, Melbourne in which most of the top talent for the 35th America's Cup competed. Burling won the world title. Barker was the worst performed of the Team New Zealand competitors, finishing in 26th place overall in the 84-boat fleet. However, he was in good America's Cup company — flanked in 25th overall by 2012 Olympic Gold medallist Tom Slingsby, a key member of Oracle Team USA in 2013 and 2017. One place behind Barker was Englishman Paul Goodison, 2008 Gold medallist in the Laser class and a then-recent signing for America's Cup Challenger Artemis Racing.

While Barker was keen to continue in the skipper and helmsman's role with Team New Zealand, no serious America's Cup team would have continued with a helmsman who'd already had three shots at winning the Cup — even taking into account the fact that he had twice won the Louis Vuitton Cup, and could not be blamed at all for the 2003 America's Cup loss.

Probably the biggest issue with Barker was that he had come up through monohull match-racing ranks, having placed second in the New Zealand Nationals when he was just 20 years old.

His nemesis Jimmy Spithill had progressed up a similar path. They knew all the same moves. The problem was that Spithill and his coach Philippe Presti had worked out the New Zealanders' match-racing playbook in San Francisco and scored telling blows at critical times in the starting box of the 2013 America's Cup.

Burling had minimal match-racing experience. His practice in Auckland in the AC50 had been against the Emirates Team New Zealand chase boat. In Bermuda, Burling proved to be an extremely quick thinker, who could position a boat very accurately. His starting tactics were unorthodox, and while he lost a few early on and created anguish among the non-sailing media, there was a method to his apparent madness. In the Match, he made the starting superstar Jimmy Spithill look very ordinary — it was a staggering performance by Burling.

It transpired that at their first meeting in December 2013, at Dalton's house, Burling had asked for the helmsman's role. 'My reaction was we've got a bit to go under the bridge yet, mate, but let's see where we get to,' Dalton recalled at the post-America's Cup media conference on 26 June 2017.

At the same media conference, it was revealed there had been a 'brutal review' in May 2014 and 20 action points were agreed. The overriding approach was 'to throw the ball out as far as we could and then see if we could get to it', Dalton said at the media conference. Against that backdrop, it would have been very surprising, given the risks that were being taken elsewhere, that Team New Zealand would not have opted to try the new talent they had on board. The real surprise would have been if Barker had been reappointed for a fourth shot at winning the America's Cup.

On 26 February 2015, Emirates Team New Zealand announced a team restructuring triggered by the announcement of Bermuda as the venue for the 35th Match in early December 2014. As previously signalled, the choice of Bermuda resulted in reduced revenue for the team from sponsorship and that, in turn, triggered a number of cuts within the programme — including a reduction in the number of AC45s the team would sail and some sailing positions. The team reduced its budget by $20 million as a result of the Bermuda selection.

Dean Barker was not offered a helming role in the now single-development boat programme.

Long-time tactician Ray Davies shifted to a coaching role with Emirates Team New Zealand for the 35th America's Cup. — RICHARD GLADWELL

But he was offered a new role as Performance Director and Head Coach, which filled the gap left by long-standing coach, Olympic Gold and Silver medallist Rod Davis, who had joined Artemis Racing.

If he accepted the role, Barker's sailing career would take a new direction as he would act as a mentor to Burling and move firmly into the Emirates Team New Zealand management team.

The sailing crew list was not announced, but it was obvious that there would be substantial change as all but two of the sailing crew from the 2013 AC72 would be aged over 40 years old by the time of the 2017 Match.

Given that, after the Black Friday media conference, the team would not hold further media sessions, the role offered to Barker was made public by an emailed media release,

advising that the team would be fully operational from Monday, 2 March 2015, from its Halsey Street base.

The team also announced it had completed the restructuring process that came out of the team-wide review after San Francisco and 50 people had signed on and would be working full-time from early March 2015. The release went on to advise that Glenn Ashby had been appointed Sailing Director and he and Peter Burling would take on helming duties.

'Dean Barker was involved in the review and restructuring process, and Emirates Team New Zealand wants to retain his services as Performance Manager and Sailing Coach with a place on the Executive Committee,' the written statement said.

'In the review of Emirates Team New Zealand, the team clearly identified the need for such a role. It is a crucial position for the team, and we have been discussing this as a possible option for Dean since last November.

'Emirates Team New Zealand recognises that Dean has significant experience and can make a valuable contribution. The role we have offered him would enable the team to capitalise on his skills.

'Emirates Team New Zealand has now made a formal offer to Dean which he is still considering.

'It should be noted that the announcement of Bermuda as the venue for the next America's Cup series had a serious impact on the team's finances and sponsorship funding, reducing the budget by some $20 million.

'This meant the team has had to reduce its remuneration budget and each team member has, as a result, taken a significant pay cut.

'Additionally, several million dollars has been axed from the operations budget leading to the scrapping of one of the foiling AC45s that we had planned and, consequently, the elimination of one of the planned helmsman positions.'

Just over a week later, then Emirates Team New Zealand Chairman Keith Turner confirmed that Dean Barker had decided not to accept the position offered to him. There was a clear point of difference in perception of the role offered. Barker believed it was largely a desk job and he wanted an active role on the water.

Emirates Team New Zealand management saw the job as being mostly on the water, albeit in the main tender. Of course, Barker would have been a very handy helmsman to step into Burling's place in case of sickness or injury, and act as a fill-in while Burling and Tuke were away in the Olympic Regatta and preliminaries side-stepping America's Cup World Series regattas.

(In mid-December 2016, the role originally intended for Barker was filled with two coaches — then five-time America's Cup winner Murray Jones and Barker's close friend and long-time tactician Ray Davies.)

On 8 May 2015 it was announced that SoftBank Team Japan had been accepted as an entry by America's Cup Event Authority, the event and marketing arm of Golden Gate Yacht Club. The challenge was made through the Kansai Yacht Club. The Japanese challenger had a partnership with the Defender Oracle Team USA under which the teams shared design and performance information. It was the first time in America's Cup history that the Defender had collaborated to such an extent with a challenger, and this created a lot of adverse comment among Cup aficionados.

Two weeks later, on 22 May 2015, SoftBank

SoftBank Team Japan's Dean Barker was joined by several former members of Emirates Team New Zealand's sailing and design teams. — GETTY

Team Japan announced that Dean Barker had agreed to join as skipper and CEO in a deal brokered by Oracle Team USA CEO Russell Coutts.

Barker and SoftBank Team Japan General Manager Kazuhiko Sofuku, known as 'Fuku', started the team from scratch, which as a kick-starter was loaned one of Oracle Team USA's early AC45S development boats. The team's America's Cup Class yacht was built by Oracle Team USA's builder, Core Builders Composites, in Warkworth, north of Auckland.

Several other former Team New Zealand sailors and shore crew joined SoftBank Team Japan, including former technical director Nick Holroyd who had been with the New Zealand team since 2000. In Bermuda, there were four New Zealanders with solid America's Cup experience in the sailing team, plus British Olympic Silver medallist Chris Draper, who came across from Luna Rossa.

SoftBank Team Japan finished fifth in the America's Cup Qualifiers of six teams and performed creditably against Artemis Racing in the Playoff Semi-Final before going down 5–3.

Once eliminated from the America's Cup regatta, Barker and his team trained with Oracle Team USA as part of their partnership agreement.

'We've had a great relationship with Oracle,' Barker said at his final media conference, 'due to the fact that they provided us with our design and everything else that goes with that. Our intention is to go and do some more sailing with them and continue with the development process.'

As for his future, Barker, who was the oldest helmsman in the regatta, replied, 'I've always enjoyed racing, and I would love to keep racing. If there is an opportunity, then I will, and we will have to see what the future does hold.'

Reflecting on his 22-year America's Cup career, Barker said, 'I have been very fortunate to be involved with some great people over the years. But history is history, and you have got to be able to move on. It has been a fantastic honour and privilege to be able to be involved in running a new team and assembling a great group of people, and I wouldn't trade that for anything.'

SoftBank Team Japan leads Artemis Racing (Sweden) in the Semi-Finals of the 2017 America's Cup Regatta.

Chapter 7

'Patrizio, we just shrank the boat!'

The 35th America's Cup featured many novel ideas. One of these was to hold the Qualifier Series or the first phase of the Challenger Selection Series in a different country to where the America's Cup Match was held.

Owned by the Oatley family, Hamilton Island Yacht Club — the original Challenger of Record for the 2017 America's Cup — is based on Hamilton Island, part of the Whitsundays in the Great Barrier Reef, almost 900 km north of Brisbane. Regatta Director for the 34th America's Cup Iain Murray is the Oatleys' long-time go-to man, having had a long and close association with the Australian winemaking family through their supermaxi, and multiple Sydney to Hobart winner, *Wild Oats*.

Luna Rossa (Italy) launch their AC72 for the 34th America's Cup in Auckland's Westhaven Marina in October 2012. — RICHARD GLADWELL

Having had their Letter of Challenge accepted by Golden Gate Yacht Club, the Oatleys' Hamilton Island Yacht Club as a valid Challenger of Record had to negotiate the Protocol to govern the 35th Match.

In an interview with Sail-World.com in early May 2014, six months after their challenge was lodged, and a month before the Protocol was released, Iain Murray was reluctant to discuss publicly how the Challenger Selection Series (CSS) would be run. The series itself, or Louis Vuitton Cup, is traditionally sailed in its entirety at the venue for the America's Cup. But a reported comment from the Defender was that maybe only the final four challenger teams would be able to sail in the America's Cup venue.

That report caused alarm and consternation among the potential challenger teams, as those who had not made the Semi-Final cut would be heading home. That's a tricky downside to have to explain to your potential sponsors whose exposure and VIP benefits would be considerably diminished if the team didn't even make it to the America's Cup venue.

Although he wouldn't name names, Murray could rattle off a contact list of 10 teams by nationality who had been in touch with him expressing interest in competing in the next America's Cup.

Emirates Team New Zealand had been the Challenger or Defender in the last five multi-challenger America's Cup Matches. They were at very short odds to take one of those final four challenger spots. That left three to be contested among the other teams — a somewhat edgy prospect, given that a challenger budget was probably going to be around $50–70 million. This amount was going to be difficult to justify if a new team was eliminated four months before the start of the second phase of the Challenger Selection Series and without being part of the hoopla associated with the Match venue.

Murray wouldn't speculate on the shape of the qualification process, except to say, 'There is flexibility on how the event may be split depending on the number of entries.

'This has been a much-debated part of the negotiations, and until the Protocol is released, it's probably better that I say no more.'

A month later in early June 2014, the Protocol was made public. Five weeks later in mid-July, Hamilton Island Yacht Club withdrew as the Challenger. They had until 8 August to confirm

The late Bob Oatley (left), Oracle Team USA's Jimmy Spithill and Team Australia's Iain Murray at Hamilton Island. — ANDREA FRANCOLINI

their entry but opted for an early bail-out.

'This challenge has grown to the point where the gap between the commercial side and the competitive costs are out of HIYC's comfort zone,' Murray told Sail-World.

'The Cup campaign has grown into a far bigger cost and potential risk, with which they [HIYC] are not comfortable,' he added.

The two-venue plan had been a contentious issue, on a number of fronts.

'I don't think that anyone favours the split venue. With a large number of challengers (in a match venue with limited space), it makes some sense. But it certainly adds cost to the campaign.'

Under the Deed of Gift which governs the America's Cup, the Defender Golden Gate Yacht Club (which has both a race team: Oracle Team USA, and an event/marketing arm: America's Cup Event Authority) has the right to name the venue for the America's Cup Match and effectively the venue for the Challenger Selection Series as well.

After Hamilton Island Yacht Club had advised that they would not be continuing with the challenge, the mantle of Challenger of Record fell to the next-entered challenger, Circolo della Vela Sicilia (CVS) and their team Luna Rossa.

In October 2014, as we have seen, the Italians gave up their right of approval, as Challenger of Record, of any change to the Protocol and turned over that right to the Challenger Committee (comprising all challenger teams), meaning that any changes to the Protocol required only the support of the majority of the challengers and the approval of the Defender.

It was a magnanimous gesture that in six months would see the Italians exit the America's Cup.

Fast forward to the third week of November 2014 and the hot tip was that Bermuda had been selected as the venue for the 35th America's Cup.

Emirates Team New Zealand CEO Grant Dalton responded to the unconfirmed reports that Bermuda had won the right to host the Cup, saying that the Kiwi team had not been told of a decision.

'We have been invited to a press conference to be held in New York on December 2 when the announcement will be made. Until then it is only media speculation.

'San Diego and Bermuda are the only potential venues left in the race so the media has a 50/50 chance of being right,' he said.

Two weeks later in early December 2014 at a media session in Manhattan, New York, America's Cup Commissioner General Harvey Schiller announced Bermuda as the America's Cup venue. Schiller also dropped into the announcement that negotiations were under way for a major event to be held in New Zealand.

Grant Dalton would not be drawn on specifics and said discussions were at an early stage. 'I hope we can pull it off. It would be great for New Zealand, for the industry, for the fan base and the team as well.'

It transpired that the event was hosting the two-week-long America's Cup Qualifier Series, rather than a round of the shorter (usually one weekend) America's Cup World Series, which hadn't ventured outside the northern hemisphere.

At the time of the announcement there were five challengers with two more said to be pending, according to the America's Cup Event Authority. If the series was confirmed, all teams would set up in Auckland.

Potentially the Qualifier Series would have more economic impact than the America's Cup itself — being of longer duration and with more teams and support staff.

Auckland's substantial marine industry facilities would have reduced the cost for teams — avoiding the need to set up facilities capable of coping with every conceivable eventuality. The event would attract substantial media coverage, both in the build-up and in the Qualifiers — which are the equivalent of the round-robin series of the former Louis Vuitton Cup. (In Auckland in 2000 and 2003 the round robin had run for six weeks.)

If Oracle Team USA exercised their right

The top portion of the letter sent to the America's Cup Commercial Commissioner confirming Auckland's host bid for the Qualifiers.

to compete, it would be the first and only time that the challengers as a group would come up against the Defender ahead of the Match, since 1970 when the first multiple challenges were accepted.

The first indication that something was awry came when the Protocol requirement that the Qualifiers venue be announced on 15 February was not met and would not be made for a further fortnight.

Auckland's bid to host the Qualifiers was all but confirmed on that same day by the New Zealand Prime Minister, John Key. The government investment was justified on the expenditure that would be brought to New Zealand by teams and fans, plus the commercial boost for New Zealand's marine industry, the export component of which relies heavily on the international shop window afforded by

Emirates Team New Zealand
PO Box 91499, Victoria Street West, Auckand, New Zealand
www.etnzblog.com

14th February 2015

Harvey Schiller
Commercial Commissioner
Americas Cup Event Authority

Dear Harvey

Re Americas Cup Qualifiers

Team New Zealand Limited, currently trading as Emirates Team New Zealand ("ETNZ") hereby confirms its bid for Auckland to be the Host City and Venue for the 35th Americas Cup Qualifiers as described in Article 2 of the Protocol governing the 35th Americas Cup ("Protocol")

involvement in the America's Cup.

As word of the Qualification Series crept across the Tasman, Australian promoters made a late bid for the Qualifiers, originally tagged for the Lucky Country.

Promoter Tony Cochrane was tipped to be involved. He'd had a colourful history and involvement with V8 Supercar series and other major events on either side of the Tasman. But it transpired that the New South Wales bid would require six to eight weeks to be scrutinised by public authorities.

Already the matter had turned into a political football with a state election looming, and Opposition politicians accusing the State Premier of 'being asleep at the wheel'. The potential Australian bid created a lot of noise but went nowhere.

It seemed that the British, French and Swedish teams were reluctant to come to New Zealand or indeed the southern hemisphere and would prefer to stay in Bermuda, to where they would relocate from their home bases in Europe or the USA.

The two strongest teams in the 2013 event in San Francisco — the Defender, Oracle Team USA and Team New Zealand — were believed to be in favour of the trip Down Under.

Oracle Team USA has a significant investment in Warkworth-based Core Builders Composites. Hot-staging Oracle Team USA's first (and maybe second) AC62 from that facility would have been a very attractive option.

The same idea of Oracle relocating to New Zealand's Northland province for their boat launch had gained traction ahead of the 2013 America's Cup but came to naught. In hindsight, given their calamitous nosedive in October 2012 in San Francisco, when they could have

been sailing off Whangarei, it might not have been a bad idea.

The date and venue of the Qualifiers were also vital as under other provisions of the Protocol teams could not sail against each other except at the venue of the Qualifiers. Other dates in the series of events that comprised the America's Cup Regatta hinged around the Qualifier dates.

Long story short was that there was a lot that should have happened but hadn't.

On Thursday, 26 March 2015, America's Cup organisers issued a media release following a competitors' conference believed to have been held the previous Monday. The thrust of the release was to repeat the mantra of reducing costs by using a smaller boat for the event.

It would seem that five of the six teams currently entered were in favour of a smaller boat than the 62-ft AC62 which had been announced as the America's Cup Class nine months previously. The team most affected was the Challenger of Record, Luna Rossa, who was well advanced in terms of having set up a base in Cagliari, Italy and had engaged a nearly full team of more than 80 people. The Italians were well down the track with AC62 design and development.

Also affected but less advanced was Oracle Team USA who had completed an AC62 wingsail plug in their Warkworth build facility.

The first cost reduction proposal to go to a single 45-ft wingsailed foiling catamaran as the America's Cup Class had a very hollow ring because several of the teams were running multiple AC45S (45-ft) development boats, which were not cheap.

Reducing salaries would have had a more significant effect — with 60 per cent of an

America's Cup campaign cost being the cost of sailors, designers and shore staff. That decision was in the hands of the individual teams. It was never explained why a change of class, nine months after it had been announced, was the best way of fixing a problem the teams had created for themselves by over-generous salary payments.

In one of several Californian State court cases following the 2013 America's Cup, it transpired that a grinder had been offered US$25,000 a month plus US$4000 Bermuda accommodation allowance (close to US$350,000 or NZ$500,000 per year). There would seem to have been more scope in the remuneration area for cost reduction than in shrinking the boat.

The media release from America's Cup organisers read: 'The competitors and organizers of the 2017 America's Cup are planning to implement a series of rule changes to dramatically reduce team operational costs, primarily by racing in a smaller boat.

'After reviewing prototypes of the new AC45S development boats being tested on the water over the past several months, it is clear that if we raced smaller boats in 2017, we could dramatically reduce costs without sacrificing any of the spectacle or the design, engineering and athletic challenge fundamental to the America's Cup.

'We have a responsibility to think of what is best for the long-term health of the America's Cup as well as improving the value equation for team principals and partners. Racing a smaller boat in 2017 and beyond is a big step in the right direction.

'The existing operational costs of teams is much too high with a boat like the AC62. We discussed making this change early last year at a Competitors Meeting in London, but at that stage, only Oracle Team USA and Emirates Team New Zealand were in favour of using a smaller boat.

'But now that the teams have seen these new boats in action there is a clear majority of competitors who support the idea. I'd like to be able to say we have unanimous support from all the teams, but that is not the case.'

The vote on the changes was to take place before the end of March.

Matters deteriorated very rapidly from there, triggered by a statement from the Luna Rossa challenge that they would consider withdrawing from the Cup if there were a change to the class of boat to be used. The Italians said any vote to change class had to be unanimous, not a simple majority of challengers with the approval of the Defender.

Of course, if they had not handed over their prerogative of approval (veto) of any Protocol change less than six months earlier, Luna Rossa would have just been able to give the idea the thumbs down, and that would have been the end of the matter.

Emirates Team New Zealand backed the Italian position by a message in social media, with the same reasoning — that teams had progressed too far down the AC62 design and planning path. It was too late to switch to a smaller boat.

After the Kiwis' position was put into social media, the Commercial Commissioner for the America's Cup, General Schiller, responded by withdrawing an agreement that had been negotiated between Emirates Team New Zealand Board member Sir Stephen Tindall and Sir Russell Coutts and signed by Schiller.

Unfortunately for America's Cup Event

Authority, Emirates Team New Zealand had a signed agreement confirming that the America's Cup Qualifiers would be held in Auckland, and they responded by publishing the header and signature pages of the letter, showing General Schiller signing for ACEA.

The withdrawal of the Qualifiers was the opening shot from Schiller. The second came when US media contacted ACEA.

Top US-based America's Cup correspondent Bernie Wilson, writing in San Diego for the Associated Press, reported:

'A few hours later America's Cup Commercial Commissioner Harvey Schiller notified Team New Zealand that a qualifying regatta in early 2017 will not be awarded to Auckland.

'While there were a number of reasons, Schiller told the Associated Press the biggest was Team New Zealand "bouncing back and forth on support" for the unprecedented mid-course [class] downsizing.

'Team New Zealand boss Grant Dalton told the AP he felt that was a negotiating ploy. However, Team New Zealand's government funding is triggered by economic value, including an Auckland regatta.

'Asked if that could be the end of the Kiwi team, Dalton said he wants to wait and see how

Decorated Vietnam combat pilot Brigadier-General Dr Harvey Schiller was Commercial Commissioner for the 35th America's Cup, resigning in August 2016.

next week plays out.

'Organisers said Wednesday that changes are being drafted, and teams will be asked to vote early next week.

'Dalton said that while the Kiwis support cost reduction, they're "completely in line with Prada" and feel any decision on boat downsizing should be unanimous.

'Dalton has sparred in recent years with Russell Coutts, a fellow Kiwi, who is both

Yours sincerely

Kevin Shoebridge
Chief Operating Officer / ETNZ

signed :

Harvey W Schiller
Commercial Commissioner
Americas Cup Event Authority

Signature portion of the letter sent to the America's Cup Commercial Commissioner confirming Auckland's host bid for the Qualifiers.

CEO of Oracle Team USA and director of the America's Cup Event Authority.

'Asked about the chance Team New Zealand could be forced to drop out, Coutts said: 'We've got everyone's interests to consider, not just one team.'

The battle lines were drawn for an apocalyptic Competitors Meeting.

Late in the afternoon of 26 March 2015 (NZT) Emirates Team New Zealand released a short video where Grant Dalton said that the team supported the position taken by Luna Rossa, because they believed it was too late to make a change to the boat and the rules, unless all teams agreed. In the video, Dalton said that the previous Saturday the teams were presented

with two deals by ACEA. One was to reduce the boats to AC45s — being 45-ft wingsailed, foiling catamarans — which would reduce costs, and have no Qualifiers in Auckland which might further reduce costs for teams. The alternative was to stay with the AC62 that had been agreed in the Protocol and have a Qualifier Series sailed in Auckland. In other words, stay with the status quo.

The 35th America's Cup appeared to be on a course to go ahead in Bermuda, without two of the most significant challengers — Luna Rossa and Emirates Team New Zealand — unless cooler heads prevailed within the Cup organisation. The loss of both the Italian and Kiwi teams would have weakened the regatta to a point where there would be a massive blow to the credibility and stature of the event — along with the loss of very significant TV audiences in Italy and New Zealand.

Luna Rossa revealed stunning graphics on their AC72 when she was launched in Auckland in October 2012. — RICHARD GLADWELL

On 2 April (NZT), the America's Cup Event Authority announced that the majority of the Cup teams had agreed to make changes aimed at significantly reducing costs for the 2017 America's Cup. Central to these changes, the ACEA said, was the introduction of an exciting new America's Cup Class — a wingsailed, foiling catamaran between 45 and 50 feet.

A check of the voting schedule showed that the two most experienced teams in the competition, Luna Rossa and Emirates Team New Zealand, had not supported the amendment to drop the AC62. The majority of the teams had also indicated a preference that all of the racing in the 2017 America's Cup be conducted at a single venue, Bermuda.

Team New Zealand posted on social media that they had filed for a hearing before the yet to be formed Arbitration Panel on the Qualifier Series issue and would be continuing to work with ACEA and the competitors to bring the Qualifiers to Auckland. The statement referred only to the Qualifiers venue issue and did not mention the change of boat/rule for the event.

On 3 April (NZT), Luna Rossa and their patron Patrizio Bertelli issued a statement confirming their withdrawal, which said in part:

'Following a careful evaluation of the serious implications of this unprecedented initiative, Team Luna Rossa confirms that it will withdraw from the 35th America's Cup.

'Team Luna Rossa indeed considers illegitimate the procedure adopted and founded on an evident abuse of process by surreptitious use of procedures to modify the Protocol in order to overturn the Class Rule, which instead requires the unanimity of the teams entered.

'It is important to underline the fact that Luna Rossa frequently advanced proposals aimed at containing costs that however would not have changed the nature of the boats, but these proposals have systematically been rejected by the Defender.

'Team Luna Rossa has also taken into consideration the possibility to protest through the Arbitration Panel as foreseen by the Protocol; it has however noted that, ten months after signing the Protocol, the Defender is only now initiating the first formal procedures to compose this important body. This fact contributes to making the entire governance of the Event even less credible and reliable.

'Patrizio Bertelli said: "I want to thank the whole team for its hard work during this past year; regretfully this effort has been frustrated by this manoeuvre that is unprecedented in the history of the America's Cup.

'"However, in sports, as in life, one cannot always go for compromise, after compromise, after compromise; sometimes it is necessary to make decisions that are painful but must be clear cut, as only these can make everybody aware of the drifts of the system and therefore set the basis for the future: respect of legality and sportsmanship".'

Emirates Team New Zealand expressed their sadness at the Italian move.

America's Cup Commissioner General Schiller issued a statement, which in part expressed disappointment at Luna Rossa's intention to withdraw.

Although there was adverse reaction from many quarters and commentators, there was no further action from the parties directly involved.

It had taken just one utterance on social media by Emirates Team New Zealand supporting the Italian stance over voting for the proposed change in class for ACEA to rip up the Auckland Qualifiers hosting agreement.

SoftBank Team Japan was accepted as an entry in the first week of May 2015, and two weeks later it was announced that Dean Barker would be the skipper and CEO of the new team.

The change of class didn't alter the number of teams in the America's Cup. It did lose one well-established four-time challenger and replaced them with one start-up team. Maybe it also helped keep the French team in the regatta, who were the first to be eliminated.

Almost 12 months later, on 20 May 2016, America's Cup Event Authority CEO Russell Coutts revealed during an interview with Sail-World's Asian Editor Guy Nowell at the Bremont sponsorship launch in Hong Kong that the Arbitration Panel would hold its first hearing in July 2016. This was the first official indication that the three-person panel had even been formed, but Sail-World's sources indicated that it had been empanelled since January 2016, possibly earlier.

The composition of the panel was never published, except that Sail-World was told that Yachting Australia President Matt Allen was one of the three members. Allen is a former investment banker and owner/skipper of *Ichi Ban* and a veteran of 25 Sydney to Hobart races. The others came from the USA and Spain. One, most likely the USA member, had to be an arbitrator listed by the Court of Arbitration for Sport.

The Arbitration Panel took over many of the functions of the World Sailing-appointed International Jury, used in the 2013 America's Cup.

Making an application or complaint to the Arbitration Panel required a US$25,000 (NZ$35,700) fee, increasing to US$100,000 (NZ$143,000) if the applicant had previously lost two applications. Justice came at a price in the 35th America's Cup.

Golden Gate Yacht Club's team, Oracle Team USA, had fallen foul of the International Jury during the previous America's Cup, being levied a US$250,000 fine, deducted 2 points in the America's Cup Match, and had several team members suspended after four measurement incidents. The Defender unusually lost three protests in the jury room.

For the America's Cup in Bermuda the International Jury's role was split between a three-man Arbitration Panel and a Jury drawn from the regatta umpires, which handled on-the-water and racing issues.

It would be 16 months before Emirates Team New Zealand's complaint was heard — and just five months before the earliest launch date for the first AC50 wingsailed catamarans. It was hard to see how the Arbitration Panel could practically order the Qualifier Series to be moved back to Auckland.

The obvious remedy was financial compensation if it was found that the Auckland-based team did have a valid hosting agreement with ACEA. However, for Emirates Team New Zealand, even compensation at the level of $10–20 million was too late to be of any use to the team, except to pay off bridging finance and backing that had to be put in place in short order for the team to survive.

The financial recompense would not compensate for the disruption caused by having to cut back from a two-boat sailing team, and a multiple development boat programme now enjoyed by several of the other challenger teams and Defender.

Quite how much of the Arbitration Panel

appointment, proceedings and decisions make it into the public purview still remains to be seen. In previous Cups, there has been limited reporting permitted of any hearings, with summaries of the proceedings being issued by the International Jury during or at the end of the hearing.

Previously, the appointment of key officials has been handled promptly and openly. This time the composition of the Arbitration Panel has been kept secret and was never publicly announced.

On 9 June 2016, the majority of competitors voted to bring in even more draconian confidentiality provisions over the operation of the Arbitration Panel. No competitor could let it be known that they had even taken a case to the Panel, let alone disclose what it was about.

The first meeting of the Panel is believed to have taken place in London in late July 2016 around the time of the second America's Cup World Series event in Portsmouth.

In all other sailing events, the competitors involved in a protest hearing are publicly known, the members of the jury or protest committee are known, the date of the hearing is posted on a club or regatta noticeboard, the subject matter of the protest is known, and the details of the decision and any penalty are posted on the same noticeboard. The Arbitration Panel and its hearing followed none of this process.

America's Cup organisers decided to place themselves above all that, implementing an adjudication system similar in concept to the modern-day 'star chamber' or crime commission created in some western judicial

The Arbitration Panel hold a hearing in Auckland in 2002. The hearings were open to observers and media representatives.

systems to combat serious high-level crime. In these commissions, witnesses are prohibited from telling anyone about the hearing or that they appear before the court. Disclosure is treated as a contempt of court, with penalty of imprisonment. The star chamber, of course, held its hearings in complete secrecy.

That extreme process might be appropriate for dealing with terrorists, drug lords and criminal masterminds — but the America's Cup? Really?

In the America's Cup context, the same disclosure prohibitions are in place, but fines and penalties ranging up to a million dollars or more take the place of imprisonment.

In early September 2016, Harvey Schiller, Commissioner for the America's Cup, confirmed his departure from the America's Cup Event Authority with a short message on his Facebook page. His last day was apparently 31 August 2016.

'For those who might not have heard, I decided to leave America's Cup after five years of service. It's been a great experience with many special people. Many new things ahead.'

Ten days earlier he had posted the cryptic comment: 'If you tell the truth, you'll remember what you said.'

Although Schiller was appointed in 2014, he had been in an advisory capacity to ACEA for three years before that — for the 34th America's Cup. ACEA did not even issue a pithy media statement in the style normally issued in such a departure, or on his replacement. For someone of Schiller's standing and integrity, it was a very telling omission.

That lack of public comment by ACEA on Schiller's departure was the giveaway that all had not gone well in the hearing — which was largely over whether Schiller had signed an agreement that was binding between ACEA and ETNZ.

The indication was that the Arbitration Panel had ruled in favour of Emirates Team New Zealand over the withdrawal of the Qualifiers from Auckland and reallocation of that event in Bermuda. As yet, the decision of the three-man Arbitration Panel has still not been published. The proceedings of the Arbitration Panel were made confidential in a Protocol change agreed by a majority of the teams on 20 June 2016 — just five or six weeks before the hearing the following month.

Simply, all the markers pointed in the same direction — to an Arbitration Panel decision in favour of Team New Zealand. That being so, it seemed that the Kiwis had little fault in the sorry saga. Complicit or not, the other challengers were beneficiaries of the windfall created by the Team New Zealand upset in April 2015.

In a second phase, the Arbitration Panel, having decided in favour of Emirates Team New Zealand, met again to consider the amount of financial compensation to be awarded. As with the first decision of the Panel, that amount has not been publicly revealed.

For all the time-consuming adversity, the longest established and most successful team in America's Cup history was able to regroup and revert to the single-development boat, single-challenger model which had seen them arrive in San Francisco in 2013 with a substantially faster yacht.

Against all odds they did the same again in 2017.

Emirates Team New Zealand sent their AC50, chase boat and other gear by Emirates Sky Cargo from Auckland to Bermuda, April 2017.

Chapter 8

Pumping pedals — the Cup campaign begins

For almost all of its 30-year America's Cup history, Emirates Team New Zealand has been one of the first to launch a boat in the new America's Cup cycle. Except for the 35th America's Cup — when they were one of the last.

That statistic underscores the fact that Emirates Team New Zealand had been forced into running quite a different sailing programme from the other teams and indeed what it had run in seven of its eight previous America's Cup campaigns.

The 30-year-old team had been given the green light to go ahead and challenge after a review by the team and Board in May 2014. The brutal review had identified 20 key points

or strategies for the team arising from the near-miss in 2013.

Entries closed for the 2017 America's Cup Regatta on 8 August 2014, and uncharacteristically the Royal New Zealand Yacht Squadron didn't lodge the challenge until the final day.

That was a harbinger of the team's precarious financial situation. Emirates Team New Zealand was running very tight on cash flow due to a combination of higher than expected entry fees and bond (US$3 million) and earlier than usual payment date, without any sponsorship flowing in, or even signed.

There were big changes ahead for the team which would shed all but one of its 2013 sailing team, lose its long-serving coach and technical director and come within a few hours of closing down completely.

One of the early losses was coach and

Emirates Team New Zealand developed the cycle grinders over three years to provide the onboard system hydraulic power. — RICHARD GLADWELL

Olympic Gold and Silver medallist Rod Davis, who had been with the team for a decade and was now into his twelfth America's Cup campaign.

Davis was first approached to work with Artemis in March 2014. 'I had some good talks with Team New Zealand after the last Cup in December. We knew we were going to part ways at that point. The split was very amicable. I got a note of congratulations from Shoebs [COO Kevin Shoebridge]. We're all good mates, but it was time for a change.

'Money didn't have anything to do with it. It is good for me to have new challenges. It is good for Team New Zealand to have a new voice, telling them a new way of looking at it. Ten years is a long time.' [Davis rejoined ETNZ briefly in mid-December, 2016.]

With no clear plan possible until the shape of the America's Cup Regatta was disclosed, Emirates Team New Zealand kept race sharp and built a solid base of foiling experience by contesting events such as the International A-class catamaran World Championships at Takapuna. There, skipper Glenn Ashby won his eighth world title in the 18-ft catamaran with team members taking four of the top five places overall. Artemis Racing skipper Nathan Outteridge (Australia) was sixth in the 18-ft foiling singlehander.

There was no America's Cup World Series operating in 2014. The New Zealand America's

Peter Burling finished third in the International A-class Worlds held in February 2014 at Takapuna Boating Club. — RICHARD GLADWELL

Cup team sailed in the Extreme Sailing Series, placing fourth overall after sailing in seven of the eight events. Alinghi, their nemesis from the 2003 and 2007 America's Cups, won the 2014 series sailed in non-foiling 40-ft catamarans on tight stadium courses. The Kiwis were the only 2017 America's Cup team to compete on the ESS circuit.

Peter Burling and Blair Tuke continued with their Olympic 49er campaign, winning the World and European Championships every year to the 2016 Olympics where they won the Gold medal. They were also named Rolex Sailors of the Year in 2015 for the clean sweep of wins in the 49er class and topping the leaderboard on the America's Cup World Series, that year.

Five members of the Emirates Team New Zealand sailing team contested the 2015 International Moth Worlds in Sorrento, near Melbourne, sailing in both the Australian and then the World Championships. This time there was a classier fleet with several America's Cup sailors, Olympic medallists and world champions among the 160 entries in the 11 ft-long singlehanded foiler.

Sailing in early January, Dean Barker, Glenn Ashby, Ray Davies, Peter Burling and Blair Tuke again came up against Artemis Racing's Nathan Outteridge.

Burling gave the fleet a sailing lesson, winning nine of the 14 races sailed. At 24 years old Burling held the 49er World and European Championships and the International Moth World titles.

In early December 2014, the venue of the next America's Cup, Bermuda, was announced 14 months after the end of the 34th Match. For Golden Gate Yacht Club, a US$15 million event fee and other undertakings amounting to over US$50 million, plus a willing government, had tipped the decision the way of the British Overseas Territory.

Bermuda was not an attractive venue to several of Emirates Team New Zealand's sponsors, and the team was forced to slash budgets by 20 per cent — a rare occurrence in America's Cup campaigns, where budget escalations of that magnitude are the norm. The cuts had to be made very carefully to avoid compromising the success of the campaign. Essentially that meant that the team had to adopt a similar one-development boat, one-race boat style of the last two campaigns — which was a higher-risk option, given that both had gone close but failed to win the America's Cup.

At the time of the Bermuda venue announcement, the delicate prospect of the Qualifiers being sailed in Auckland was still being negotiated and signed off — which would have secured funding from several government agencies.

Originally the team strategy, born out of the May 2014 review, was to have a twin AC45 development programme with Burling at the helm of one and Dean Barker on the other. That would have provided a vital check and balance on the vexed crew selection issue, and enabled boat upgrades checked on the water boat against boat, rather than boat against the computer. With two AC45S boats and crews, they could gain vital match-racing practice, with the experienced Barker-led crew pitched against the more flamboyant and unorthodox style of Yachting New Zealand's NZL Sailing Team.

After the decision for the Match to be sailed in Bermuda, the two boats were cut back to just one AC45S boat and crew. Dean Barker was not reappointed as skipper. The new strategy was a much higher risk, but the team had to live within its budgets and it would require careful management with no mistakes.

In a statement issued by the team in late February 2015, the role of team skipper appeared to have been abolished, and helming duties were to be shared between wingsail trimmer, A-Class World Champion Glenn Ashby and 49er World and International Moth Champion Peter Burling.

At that stage, Emirates Team New Zealand had re-signed several of the crew from the 2013 campaign — Ray Davies, Jeremy Lomas, Winston Macfarlane and Derek Seward — and with Burling and Tuke aboard there was a good mix of fresh but Olympic-hardened thinking and school of hard knocks America's Cup experience.

As we know, Barker declined the Performance Coaching role that Emirates Team New Zealand had offered, and took up an offer three months later to be helmsman, skipper and CEO with the new SoftBank Team Japan. Lomas, Macfarlane and Seward joined him, leaving a big hole in the sailing team. They were also joined by long-serving technical director Nick Holroyd.

Emirates Team New Zealand's 2017 campaign started in earnest on Monday, 2 March 2015, with the team swelling to 50 full-time staff — half that of the 2013 campaign at its peak. The 20-strong design team that had been running part time for a year stepped up to a full-time basis, with new design team members starting.

With a sailing team now of just four sailors, Emirates Team New Zealand embarked on a crew search and selection ahead of the first regatta in the America's Cup World Series, staged in Portsmouth, England in late July 2015.

After not winning the 34th America's Cup, there were widespread calls outside the team, in New Zealand, for new blood to be brought in. That process was started in January 2014 with the introduction of Peter Burling and Blair Tuke to the sailing squad and the forging of a partnership with Yachting New Zealand, instead of the previous distant to non-existent relationship with the national body for sailing, epitomised by the pre-2013 scrap between the two outfits over use of the stylised fern graphic on the NZL Sailing Team uniforms.

In their talent search, Emirates Team New Zealand looked to the two crews who placed first and second in the Red Bull Youth America's Cup sailed in San Francisco. Also in the viewfinder were more members of the NZL Sailing Team, and as it turned out the wider New Zealand Olympic team. Bringing new sailors without America's Cup experience into the team helped reduce the salary budget significantly.

The direct hook-up with the NZL Sailing Team (from which the Olympic team was drawn) was a first for any team in America's Cup history. It was a move which developed in all sorts of directions and exceeded all expectations — both getting Emirates Team New Zealand out of a tight spot, and providing a pathway for all young sailors to the high-profile professional sailing team.

In its promotion of the sport, Yachting New Zealand could point to most of the sailing team as having gone through its programmes — setting the ambitions of a kid that was having his first sail in an Optimist with those who were winning at Olympic and professional sailing levels. The power of that linkage cannot be overstated. However, pathway aside, the raw talent and competitive hardness to win still needs to be there in the young sailors. They don't hand out participation certificates in America's Cup racing where there is no second.

The move made a huge difference to the media profile of sailing. When competing at the 2016 Olympics, some of the shine would rub off onto the America's Cup team (in a non-America's Cup year). And when the America's Cup was being sailed (in a non-Olympic year), the Olympic sailing programme would share the America's Cup spotlight.

Sailors running in both campaigns received a salary from Emirates Team New Zealand, as well as funding from Sport New Zealand via Yachting New Zealand's High Performance Programme. Sailors still able to fit in tertiary studies were also eligible for Prime Minister's Scholarships, which at least partially funded their education. In turn, many of the sailors then undertook courses of study that were relevant to the Olympic and America's Cup programmes. Peter Burling chipped away at an engineering degree until the time demands of professional sailing took over.

The trick with the new talent, who had no previous America's Cup experience, was to get them up and beyond the standard of the other teams.

While some looked askance at the departures of experienced sailors from the team, calculations after the last America's Cup showed that only two of the sailing squad in San Francisco would be under the age of 40 by the 2017 America's Cup. Those coming on board lowered the average age to the late twenties. Emirates Team New Zealand was the youngest team in Bermuda and had a strong base for

Royal New Zealand Yacht Squadron coaches young sailors in foiling Nacra 20 catamarans as part of its High Performance Programme. — RICHARD GLADWELL

the defence in 2021, plus a conveyor belt of talent coming from Yachting New Zealand's programmes, if more talent was required.

In early October 2015 Emirates Team New Zealand came to a working arrangement with the self-exiled Luna Rossa, bringing the Italian's former skipper, the highly experienced Max Sirena, in on the operations side of the organisation. Also joining were six other members of the Luna Rossa design and sailing team.

As well as people, the Italian team loaned the New Zealand team one of their first-generation foiling AC45s. The wingsailed foiling catamaran had two major upgrades from the Italians, and

Emirates Team New Zealand gave it a third.

At ground level, the Italian–Kiwi AC45S looked very austere, despite her chic graphics. Looking down from the dock it was apparent the design team hadn't been sitting around. The former tiller-steered boat now had a hybrid wheel/tiller steering system fitted along with canting daggerboard. There was only one deck winch. A battery bank powered the boat's systems for up to six hours — an approach taken by the other teams early in their campaigns as a way of calculating energy requirements.

For the Italians, it was a sound move,

enabling them to stay abreast of America's Cup technology and sailing, and pick up some of the culture of the three-time Challenger and twice America's Cup winner. It also built on the relationship that had been established in the build-up to San Francisco and indeed going back to Auckland and the 2000 Match when Max Sirena started his Cup career as a grinder aboard the Challenger Prada.

The Kiwis' campaign hit its lowest point on 25 October 2015.

CEO Grant Dalton penned an email to the team sponsors advising: 'It is with deep regret that I wish to inform you we will be closing on the 30th of October, 2015.'

'We were closing that afternoon,' he later recalled. 'I came back to a board meeting in the afternoon and asked for them just to give me the night. I worked through and closed a deal

Emirates Team New Zealand's AC45S development boat featured a rudder gantry which extended the boat to be close to the AC50's length. — RICHARD GLADWELL

during that night which kept us going until that Christmas and then it went from there. But it has been difficult the whole time.'

In early December 2015, just 18 months before the start of the 2017 America's Cup Regatta in Bermuda, Emirates Team New Zealand took the first sailing steps with the launch and sea trial of their development AC45 on loan from Luna Rossa. Other well-funded teams were already sailing their second development boat.

After the team had been trying to find a suitable weather window for three days, the Kiwis' first sail took place under grey skies in front of early-morning commuter traffic crossing the Harbour Bridge.

After 20 years on the edge of Auckland's Viaduct Harbour — and having been the driving force behind its development — the team was forced to move out of their base to make way for a new hotel and into very austere former oil facility administration offices in Silo Park, on the edge of Auckland's Westhaven Marina.

Six months later, in the third week of June 2016, Emirates Team New Zealand celebrated a long-awaited milestone at their spartan Beaumont Street base, launching their first custom-designed development boat. The 45-ft catamaran known as an AC45S in 35th America's Cup parlance took a dedicated team of boat builders over 35,000 man hours to construct, spread over six months, at the team's base.

Finally, Emirates Team New Zealand was on their first true development boat while Artemis Racing (Sweden) and Land Rover BAR (Britain) had two and Oracle Team USA had three. SoftBank Team Japan had one passed on from the US Defender as part of their controvesial Challenger–Defender partnership arrangement.

The design trick in the new Emirates development boat was, with the addition of an extended rudder gantry at the stern, the designers had increased the effective length of the Kiwis' AC45S by about three feet. That left only a couple of feet to be soaked up in the slightly shorter bows to reach the same dimensions as the AC50 which would be used in the America's Cup, but which at that time couldn't be launched for another six months.

Hull water-line length, which determines the speed of a yacht in monohulls, doesn't have any speed effect on a foiling multihull as the hulls are flying through air, not water. The major determinant of speed in foiling multihulls is the power generated from the wingsail and the righting moment required to offset that power. So for Emirates to have hulls a couple of feet shorter than an AC50 was of no consequence — provided the same AC50-sized wingsail was used, the same foils, and the beam was the same as the AC50 — giving similar righting moment and speed.

The canny rudder design feature meant that what was supposed to be an AC45 now had the same geometry as the bigger AC50. In simple terms, there was the same distance between the foils as the America's Cup race boat, the same beam, the same wingsail, and they could run and test AC50 daggerboards and rudders.

Effectively it was an AC50, and the team had stolen a march on the other five teams, getting an additional six months' testing time in a full-size boat, before launching their race boat.

Adapted from skiff classes, the gantry was a massive piece of kit, spliced into the after sections of the AC45 hull. As it is technically part of the rudder, it flies below the rules which talk only about overall hull length, and rudders were not part of that length measurement.

Skipper Glenn Ashby was coy on whether the team's surrogate was an AC50 or AC45. 'It's an AC45 in terms of the rule, but with characteristics of an AC50. We can emulate the performance characteristics of an AC50,' he explained at the launch.

'This boat will get us from a base level of performance when launched to one where we are very close to having the right bits and pieces to make our AC50 race boat fast when she is splashed — and hopefully better than our competitors.'

With the advanced AC45S punching well above its weight, the Kiwis were now catching up the ground that had been lost by the actions of others.

The next significant move came on Christmas Eve 2016 when Emirates Team New Zealand added five-time America's Cup winner Murray Jones 'to help guide the team in the most important six months of the 35th America's Cup campaign'.

A former double Olympic representative in the Flying Dutchman class, Jones placed fifth in the 1988 Korean Olympics and fourth in 1992 in Barcelona. He was a former European champion in the 470 class and was selected for the 1980 New Zealand Olympic team in that class (which was not sent due to the boycott of the USSR).

Jones switched to the America's Cup after the 1992 Olympics, first joining Team New Zealand in 1995 for two America's Cup wins, before going to Alinghi after the 2000 America's Cup. There he was part of the team that won the 2003 and 2007 America's Cups, losing the 2010 Cup sailed in 120-ft multihulls in Valencia. He then joined Oracle Team USA for the 2013 campaign in San Francisco.

An engineer by profession, Jones was a top sparmaker before moving across into the America's Cup. Like all 470 helmsmen, Jones is relatively light in stature and with his excellent eyes and cool manner he was a frequent visitor to the towering masthead of the 75-ft monohulls whenever the input of a good wind spotter was required by the brains trust of trimmers, tactician and skipper.

Since the 2013 America's Cup, Jones had been more focused on his daughter Gemma's Rio Olympic campaign in the Nacra 17 foiling catamaran. She placed an extremely creditable fourth in the 2016 Olympics — her first Olympic campaign.

Jones worked alongside former Emirates Team New Zealand tactician Ray Davies, who had switched from the sailing team to the coaching and performance team after the departure of long-time friend Dean Barker for the Japanese team.

In mid-December 2016, six months before the America's Cup Regatta was due to start, the six America's Cup teams 'voluntarily' imposed a 28-day non-sailing blackout on themselves. The surprise move came off the back of the Arbitration Panel's still confidential decision in favour of Emirates Team New Zealand after ACEA's Commercial Commissioner General Schiller improperly cancelled the agreement to hold the America's Cup Qualifiers in Auckland, back in April 2015.

The 'voluntary' blackout amendment to the Protocol is believed to have been brokered by the three-man Arbitration Panel — giving the teams the chance to come up with their own arrangement for time compensation, rather than have the Panel do it for them. Coming two weeks before the teams were to be permitted to launch their AC50s, the blackout period was further evidence that the marketing and event management arm of the Defender, Golden Gate Yacht Club, had taken a drubbing in the July 2016 hearing in London.

The blackout period kicked in from 9 January 2017, and was clearly an arrangement to mitigate the time lost by Emirates Team New Zealand in having to ship their boat to Bermuda, while the five teams complicit in the decision to change the America's Cup Class to the AC50 kept sailing in Bermuda.

As a result of the Protocol amendment, Emirates Team New Zealand, along with the other teams, faced an unexpected strategic decision as to when to launch their America's Cup Class race boat, and like the other five teams rejigged their development programme, opting to delay the launch of their AC50 by at least a month.

Emirates Team New Zealand splashed their new AC50 in Auckland on 14 February 2017, revealing another breakthrough and what proved to be a game-changer in Bermuda.

The unheralded mid-morning launch was attended by a spy boat from Oracle Team USA with Olympic Silver medallist and America's Cup veteran Don Cowie talking animatedly on a mobile phone — presumably back to Bermuda —

The first published image of the cycling grinders aboard Emirates Team New Zealand's AC50, here waiting to have her first sail — February 2017.

— RICHARD GLADWELL

and with photographer Chris Cameron, who had been with Team New Zealand for 10 years, shooting. The pair kept Team New Zealand company while they sailed their AC50 in Auckland.

(While certain restrictions remained on reconnaissance, the former rules about not approaching within 200 metres of another competitor without permission were gone — photographers with long lenses could get very close, and no development secret was safe for long.)

Keeping tabs on Emirates Team New Zealand

There were few restrictions on reconnaissance in the 35th America's Cup. Here Oracle Team USA report to Bermuda on Emirates Team New Zealand's AC50 before her first sail. — RICHARD GLADWELL

was a simple exercise using various webcams dotted around the Viaduct and inner Waitemata Harbour which overlooked the Emirates Team New Zealand base. The webcam network saved racer-chasers an enormous amount of wasted time as the AC45/50 could be tracked from a home, office or mobile phone.

Given that the team usually took 30 to 60 minutes from when their wingsail was hoisted to when they launched, photographers had plenty of notice to get into position, ready to catch the AC45S and AC50 for a vital couple of minutes as they raced past.

With the 28-day blackout period finishing on 5 February 2017, it was relatively easy to predict the window in which Emirates Team New Zealand would launch. A week or so after the blackout window lifted the AC50's

wingsail could be seen raised for the first time between the tanks and buildings surrounding the team base in Beaumont Street.

I was going to the city for a haircut, and left 30 minutes early, grabbing my camera gear on the way out, and stopped by Westhaven Marina. There it was a very animated scene as a spy boat chartered by Oracle Team USA buzzed back and forth with Cowie and Cameron taking it all in. They were hyperactive. Behind them, Emirates Team New Zealand's AC50 sat in the water, with the grinding crew looking like they were sitting on their pedestals but, oddly enough, seeming to be quite relaxed on what should have been a very uncomfortable seat.

Haircut completed, I headed home and downloaded my photos onto a computer and could see that the grinders were sitting on top of what should have been conventional grinding stations — but their legs were bent as if on a bicycle. After flicking into zoom view, it was obvious that the grinders were, in fact, sitting on bike seats. Somehow the team had managed to keep a big secret — learning their lesson from prematurely showing off the foiling AC72 in the previous Cup cycle.

A check back with the webcam, and now the jib was hoisted — a sure sign that the AC50 was about to head out sailing. Five minutes later I was at the Devonport waterfront.

On her first sail Emirates Team New Zealand's AC50 looked very impressive — sailing in winds right on, or below, the America's Cup minimum wind limit of 6 kts with the wind at times being only 4 kts and not suitable to race conventional boats.

She did one run up the harbour. After a few seconds to build speed, she lifted onto her foils effortlessly and stayed foil borne for a kilometre or so, without touching the water. On the return run downwind, she again climbed onto her foils for two or three seconds and then stayed foiling without touchdown.

The next day the red and black AC50 did a very impressive run down the inner Waitemata from the Western Viaduct to North Head in a breeze which looked like 7–8 kts. She covered the 4-nautical-mile leg in five and a half minutes, only doing the briefest of touchdowns through a boat wake, including three foiling gybes.

Because all control systems were hydraulically driven, Emirates Team New Zealand's AC50 looked very clean and simple on her launch. — RICHARD GLADWELL

One of the features of the 35th America's Cup was the outstanding job done by Jason Smith shooting video from the shore of the various AC50s training and racing on the Great Sound, and publishing these on YouTube. His videos became a must-see for fans and teams during the America's Cup work-up sessions in Bermuda.

There is not a lot you can tell about boat speed from a video because in the wingsailed foiling multihulls a small increase in wind strength or direction can make a huge difference to speed. What you can see is the frequency of speed-robbing splashdowns, and the error rate in foiling tacks or gybes, and then compare those with a similar view of Emirates Team New Zealand on the inner Waitemata, which was a more difficult stretch of water than the Great Sound.

On all counts Emirates Team New Zealand had a vastly better performance — and, providing her speed checked in with the other teams and the Kiwi team and suppliers kept the developments coming, then the Kiwis were at very short odds to win the America's Cup.

After the last extended session of practice racing concluded in Bermuda, a couple of weeks before the start of the Qualifiers, Artemis Racing was consistently beating the Defender Oracle Team USA. It was as certain as you can ever be in yacht racing that the America's Cup was going to be changing hands at the end of June 2017.

Two days after having her first couple of sailing sessions, Emirates Team New Zealand formally christened their new AC50 America's Cup challenger on a rainy Auckland afternoon. The christening ceremonies took place in moderately heavy rain, reviving memories of the same ceremony conducted a hundred metres down Beaumont Street just over 30 years previously, when the Kiwis' first America's Cup challenger, the 12-Metre *KZ-7*, was christened by Dame Naomi James.

Members of Ngati Whatua, the local iwi, welcomed the rain, saying it was the tears of happiness of sailors' ancestors who had gathered above for the christening.

Up close the team's AC50 was noticeable for being a very aerodynamically clean boat, and other than four cycle seats and a steering wheel, little else appeared above the trampoline and deck line.

It was disclosed that the team had decided to go with the pedal option over 12 months earlier, having worked through the concept for 24 months previously. The team and those in the know had managed to keep the development under wraps for that time, including launching their AC45S test boat with conventional hand-powered grinding systems.

Emirates Team New Zealand skipper Glenn Ashby told Sail-World that the team had only sailed for the first time with the cyclors on her first sessions on the water, and the rest of the development had been undertaken on shore-based test platforms.

The Olympic Bronze medal-winning cyclist Simon van Velthooven joined the team 12 months earlier, and the team switched to a cycling-orientated physical training programme about that time.

'The team started work on the project three years ago, but the actual testing started 18 to 24 months ago,' explained skipper, wingsail trimmer and Sailing Director Glenn Ashby as the rain poured down at the launch.

'The team has done well to keep it under wraps for all this time. There have been a lot of different industries involved to help us. It has been great to have been able to keep it in the bag for as long as we did.

'It was something we had talked about as a group a long time ago. Most of the teams have looked at it, I'm sure, over the years. We were open-minded to it from Day 1 and being only a small group we agreed it was an option and ran with it from there.

'It involved resource and effort from every department within the team, along with a lot of other areas. It emerged as an option after some initial testing. With more development and learning it just kept on stepping up the priority list to look at more closely.

'Once we decided to take it on, we just went "full noise".

'We wouldn't have done it if we didn't think it had advantages over existing grinding systems. One of the advantages we saw along the way was for the guys to be able to use their hands in different functionalities on the boat instead of just on grinding pedestals. While they are putting in power, they can be doing other functions more accurately than they can do with their feet on existing grinding pedestals using floor buttons.

'Obviously, using greater power out of your legs, as opposed to your upper body, has always been on the table. Hopefully, the jig testing, the pump development and the system development that we have done will pay

The four cyclors' seats can be clearly seen as Emirates Team New Zealand's AC50 returns from a training sail on the Waitemata Harbour. — RICHARD GLADWELL

dividends and give us a bigger range of gears in the gearbox than what we could have done potentially with grinders.

'Efficiency is one of the keys to getting the boats around the track. But the boats are very underpowered as far as what you need to do, all the manoeuvres, adjusting the wing and the foils — more than once in some manoeuvres. I don't think there would be any team out there who says "we have got too much power".

'The challenge is to use as much power as you can as effectively as possible. If you have extra power and can use it efficiently then hopefully that turns to speed against your opponents — and that has been our focus.'

Ashby says the Kiwi team didn't test the cycling power on their AC45S test platform. All

testing for the viability of cycle power was done on shore, using cockpit mock-ups and wind tunnel testing.

'We did a lot of work with Cycling New Zealand early on — making sure the ergonomics were right. It is a very complex issue. I can see why other teams have dismissed it because it is complicated.

'We designed, engineered and built the system in house, but we did get a huge number of parts done externally. We did utilise a lot of our suppliers and wonderful sponsors to help us put those pieces together as a whole,' Ashby says.

'The first day of sailing was always going to be a bit of an eye-opener. We were foil taking and foil gybing on Day 1 — after structurally commissioning/testing everything. That was quite an amazing feeling to be able to pull those manoeuvres off. The first boat to ever do a foiling tack in the world with the guys on pedals!'

The cyclors on Emirates Team New Zealand pack low in Round Robin 1 to reduce windage and boat-slowing drag. — RICHARD GLADWELL

Emirates Team New Zealand had the youngest performance engineer of any team, Elise Beavis, working on the aerodynamics of the cyclors as well as beam fairing design. She came to the team straight from the University of Auckland. The final confirmation of the project came after a two-day session with the cyclists in the wind tunnel at the university.

The other half of the switch to pedal power was the physical conditioning of the crew. A vital part of that process was the hiring of Simon van Velthooven.

'We have had Simon with us for 12 months,' Ashby explained. 'He has come in as a pro cyclist and a sprinter. He set the bar for our sailing team guys to be able to get to his level power-wise. Our guys have stepped it up massively. Simon has done a lot of the testing with us and has been a great help, but I think he has got his work cut out for him as he has some guys gunning for him in the power stakes. They are all pushing some big numbers.

'The guys coming off dinghy sailing have all done a lot of cycling in the past. Our trainer was able to transition the guys from a grinding-based environment into a cycling-based environment. They have all stepped up as a group and really pushed each other hard — and then used Simon to set the bar at an Olympic level.

'We have a huge amount to learn as to how to sail the boat, but in the power stakes those guys have done a great job and will continue to get better as we go forward.

'Almost a year and a half ago we started phasing this in as part of our training programme. As we neared launch date, we tapered the training more and more into developing power in the lower half of the body. It certainly isn't something that has been left to chance or the last minute.

'The physical conditioning is not a switch you can do over a couple of months — the conditioning has to be done over a long time and, hopefully, we have done enough to be strong enough to make it work properly.'

(To put all the talk about the merits of cyclors versus arm-grinders in context there is an interesting demonstration on YouTube of a world champion sprint cyclist Robert Förstemann trying to generate sufficient cycle power to drive a 700w toaster. He succeeds doing just one lightly toasted piece!)

The very clean deck layout on the AC50 underscored the attention given to aero-drag reduction — one of the three areas of open design on the otherwise one-design boat (the others being foils and control systems).

The clean layout approach stems from ETNZ's ability to run every control system via hydraulics — which in turn is facilitated by the additional energy or pressure generated by the pedalling crew.

'On the AC72 we had a winch on the wingsail and had six guys attached to it trimming hard to move the wing and sail the boat accurately,' Ashby recalled. 'Effectively nothing has really changed here — the accuracy in the aero trimming has a huge impact on how the boat sails — you certainly use plenty of power on these boats which are real slave-ships. Hopefully, the better accuracy results in a better performance, and for accuracy you need power,' he added.

'We don't have a wing winch on this boat,' said Ashby. 'We have been hydraulic from Day 1 on the AC45S. That was because we were hopefully moving into this pedalling format.

'As a wing trimmer, I had to get used to trimming the wing differently — it was a massive learning curve for everyone. But I am glad we took it on when we did because it is quite a transition to go to a different system, and you have to teach yourself a lot of new skills.

'It is really just a different way of hanging onto a rope!

'Now it is all hydraulics — a lot of buttons and a lot of levers. If I ever have to hang up my sailing boots, I will make a pretty good excavator driver! Might be Ashby Earthmoving in a couple of years — maybe!'

At the launch, Emirates Team New Zealand's Technical Director Dan Bernasconi gave a few clues as to where he thought the differences might lie once the six teams entered in the 35th America's Cup shaped up in Bermuda.

'We have had a great run. We've had a few hiccups along the way, as always. But the boat is going really well. We are getting through manoeuvres very well. And we think our straight-line speed is good.

'But until we line up with the other guys, it is hard to know where we stack up on that,' added Bernasconi, who holds a PhD in mathematical modelling and aerodynamics. After spending six years in the heady world of F1 and the McLaren Racing team, Bernasconi came to Emirates Team New Zealand after the break-up of team Alinghi in 2010.

'There are a lot of very complex systems on the boat — wing control systems, daggerboard systems, rudder systems, and obviously we are pushing all of those as hard as we can. We haven't made life easy for ourselves, and there were always going to be some teething problems, but nothing too major. We are happy where we are at the moment.'

Addressing the trade-off between reliability and boat performance, Bernasconi said per-formance comes first. 'Our main goal is to make a fast boat that will get us through the manoeuvres. We can't afford to be relaxed on reliability, but ultimately if we lost one race because of reliability and won all the others because we had a faster boat, we'd be in good shape. Speed is more important,' he adds.

Bernasconi believed there would be several factors in play to determine the relative speeds of the six teams contesting the America's Cup Regatta.

'The appendages will be a big part of that. The real questions will be how accurately you control those appendages; how accurately you control the rudder; how accurately you can control the daggerboards and how well you can control the wing.

'Those items all tie in with power and the more power you have, the more adjustments you can make. It is a matter of getting those pieces of the puzzle together and getting through the manoeuvres.

'Each manoeuvre takes a huge amount of power — just getting the daggerboards up and down, making big rake changes on the daggerboard and again having more power available helps in that situation.'

Looking at the nuances of daggerboard design and particularly light-air and all-purpose daggerboards, Bernasconi said the chord length (the overall length measurement from the front to back of the daggerboard, or profile width) 'is a really important performance number'.

'That is something which teams have been iterating on. The chord length you choose is a trade-off between how soon you get foiling and how fast you go once you are foiling. There is a difference between the teams on that. Some teams are at the higher end of the scale on that, and that may be some of the reason why they have a slower performance in some conditions, but can be better in manoeuvres.'

Bernasconi compares the simple theory of hydrofoil performance to that of an aircraft wing. At low speeds, you are looking for a wider wing to assist with quick take-off, and at higher speeds, you want a smaller wing for lower drag and faster speed.

'It's a trade-off we look at very carefully. In the AC50, at lift-out, you need a lot of area, and as soon as you are foiling and flying, you would rather have much less area.

'In an aircraft, you have flaps which extend for the take-off and landing. We don't have that ability, so we have to work out how to take off with the least amount of area and then in a straight line make the best performance we can, given that we have too much surface area.'

Bernasconi thought that the team design development plan had run pretty much to expectations. Which begs the question as to whether the Kiwis had been able to achieve more with less?

'Everything has gone pretty much in line with our expectations. We worked very hard on simulation tools in the first part of this campaign, rather than try to develop on the water.

'So, everything on this boat has been developed through simulation — and it has tested on the water in line with our expectations.'

The question of the accuracy of that design, simulation and test programme was answered unequivocally on the waters of the Great Sound in Bermuda in June 2017.

Emirates Team New Zealand's AC50 shows the effect of the apparent windspeed — the sails are sheeted very close to the centreline regardless of wind direction. — RICHARD GLADWELL

Chapter 9

Sponsors — long-time and new

For all the issues and controversies stemming from the 2013 America's Cup, Emirates Team New Zealand proved that it had pulling power like few other sporting outfits.

In mid-April 2014, the Duke and Duchess of Cambridge took part in a match race on the Auckland harbour during a royal visit. With crowds lining vantage points around the Viaduct and the Waitemata, the Duke at the helm of *NZL-68* and the Duchess on *NZL-41* — both boats from the America's Cup monohull era — had two races on the inner harbour.

Grant Dalton called tactics for the Duke, Dean Barker for the Duchess.

The race yachts — now owned by Explore Group — were crewed by a mix of Emirates Team New Zealand members, Royal New Zealand Yacht Squadron Youth training scheme

members and young sailors from Auckland yacht clubs.

The Duke and Duchess of Cambridge charmed their fans ashore and turned in a sailing spectacle on the water — all captured by a massive international media contingent, and with images and stories sent around the world.

As happens so often in the America's Cup, the teams can generate media attention and exposure that just cannot be bought, other than by a unique combination of circumstances — a pair of America's Cup yachts, in Emirates Team New Zealand livery; an America's Cup team; the RNZYS Youth programme to bolster the crews; and the stunning Viaduct Harbour in downtown Auckland.

Emirates Team New Zealand is now the longest established and most successful professional sailing team in world sailing, and has been for some time.

'We've been on board for 14 years now. It has been an incredibly successful relationship,' Gary Chapman, President Group Services,

---

Blair Tuke carries the America's Cup through the Emirates A380 as the team flies home. Emirates Airlines have supported the team since 2004. —
CARLO BORLENGHI

Emirates Group, told Radio Live in a post-Cup interview. 'We have created what I think is one of the most incredible brands in sport, certainly in yachting, and that is Emirates Team New Zealand. It is a global brand as well as a New Zealand brand. We've built up something that is very special.

'Everything about the America's Cup and what Emirates Team New Zealand has done in terms of innovation, pushing the boat out and thinking outside the box reflects very much what we, as an airline, have done in the aviation industry. I think it is an incredibly professional outfit. It resonates with what we are all about as well,' he added.

Emirates Airlines was the first of the major

In April 2014, the Duke and Duchess of Cambridge (striped top) spent the afternoon racing International America's Cup Class yachts with Emirates Team New Zealand. — RICHARD GLADWELL

sponsors to re-sign with the America's Cup team, renewing their then 12-year relationship in mid-May 2015.

Several suppliers and sponsors have been with the New Zealand America's Cup team over its 30-year history and three renditions (1987–1992) as New Zealand Challenge, then (1992–2003) as Team New Zealand and as Emirates Team New Zealand (2003–2017).

Omega began their sponsorship relationship with then Team New Zealand back in the 1995 America's Cup with Peter Blake and have been a naming sponsor with the team for the four America's Cups since in San Diego, Valencia, San Francisco and Bermuda. They re-signed with the team for the 35th America's Cup, just over a month after Emirates, in mid to late May 2015.

Toyota has the longest ongoing relationship with the team, and probably one of the longest enduring sponsorships in sailing, having been

with the America's Cup team since the 1992 campaign in San Diego. Toyota was the third major sponsor to come back on board in June 2015. Also, Bob Field, former Toyota New Zealand managing director, joined the Board of Emirates Team New Zealand in April 2014 along with four other appointees.

Steinlager, a name synonymous with New Zealand yachting success, returned in 2017 after a 14-year break. Sir Douglas Myers, who passed away just under three months before the 35th America's Cup got under way, was a long-time backer of Sir Peter Blake. The relationship with Myers and Lion Nathan went back to the 1985–86 Whitbread Round the World Race, with Blake in *Lion New Zealand*, before Blake won the race and all six legs with *Steinlager 2* in the 1989–90 Whitbread, with *Fisher & Paykel NZ* skippered by Emirates Team New Zealand CEO Grant Dalton in second place. Kevin Shoebridge,

Emirates Team New Zealand's COO, was a watch captain on *Steinlager 2*. Steinlager has the unique honour of being a team sponsor for all three of New Zealand's America's Cup winners.

Nespresso re-signed for the 2017 America's Cup campaign after being a first-time Emirates Team New Zealand sponsor in 2013. Pirelli and Torpedo7 were first-time sponsors for the 2017 America's Cup campaign. Also behind the team is a raft of suppliers, some of whom contribute product, others their time and expertise. Since the team's inception Team New Zealand has been a shop window for the New Zealand marine industry which now has an annual revenue in excess of $1.6 billion.

The match racing with the Duke and Duchess of Cambridge attracted huge international media attention and exposure for Emirates Team New Zealand. — RICHARD GLADWELL

Chapter 10

Qualifier Series — dodgems on the Great Sound

Round Robin 1, Day 1

The Qualifiers for the 35th America's Cup got under way a day late after 30-kt winds were forecast for the time racing was due to begin. With the Opening Ceremony due to take place after the first day's racing, organisers weren't prepared to take the risk of the weather forecast being correct.

A pre-start collision in Race 6 of the opening day of the Qualifiers captured internet clickbait attention but was otherwise a distraction to the real take-outs of the opening day of the 35th America's Cup.

First of these was the outcome of the

Emirates Team New Zealand performs a staged nosedive to celebrate their win over Artemis Racing on Day 2 of Round Robin 1. — RICHARD GLADWELL

rematch of the 2013 America's Cup protagonists — Oracle Team USA and Emirates Team New Zealand, in Race 5.

The Kiwi crew showed their form in Race 3, crushing the hapless Groupama Team France by almost the length of the final run. *Aotearoa New Zealand* was on the short leg to the finish while *Groupama Team France* was completing her rounding of the windward mark for the final time.

There are no immediate or obvious answers to the French performance, other than it was a new team that started late and always had a real uphill battle to get up to speed with the established teams. Their foiling performance was not good, with more than the average number of splashdowns. After just the first day, the French performance signalled that they would be the first to be eliminated.

The Kiwis got away to a good start in Race 5 — bang on the line with speed, but with Oracle Team USA just stacked to windward. Skipper Jimmy Spithill was able to drive over and get to the first mark with a handy lead which he should have extended and maintained to the end. However, that was not to be, and the rookie crew aboard Emirates Team New Zealand, some having their first-ever yacht race, slipped through and crossed ahead on the beat.

Then it was the turn of the New Zealand crew to give the America's Cup champions a sailing lesson, which lasted right until the final mark. But the Kiwis' moderate lead was always

going to be difficult to defend if the trailing crew elected to try to get an alternate phase of the breeze. The Australian afterguard of Jimmy Spithill, Tom Slingsby and Kyle Langford performed outstandingly, got a sniff of a useful shift and once again indulged in their favourite game of turning around the Kiwis.

Having got in front, the red-headed, feisty Aussie skipper wasn't going to let the Kiwis off the hook.

The other matches did produce some surprises — or outcomes that ran against the form guide.

Land Rover BAR performed outstandingly against Artemis Racing, who from the practice sessions was expected to be the benchmark for the fleet, Defender included.

Ainslie looked like he had grown another leg and looked extremely comfortable to be

---

Land Rover BAR misjudged a turn and mounted SoftBank Team Japan in Race 6 of Round Robin 1. Both boats raced despite damage, but the Brits almost sank at the dock. — RICHARD GLADWELL

showing Artemis Racing around the 17-minute-long course.

In Race 6, Ainslie blotted his copybook for the second time with a pre-start incident in the final race of the day, when he made a misjudgement of speed and distance.

He'd done the same with Emirates in practice racing, in the 'love-tap' incident when he came from astern at the start, tried to pass between the Kiwis' and the starting mark, collecting both and putting a bow through the topside of the port hull on Emirates. Fortunately it was above the water line — but it was still a substantial repair task for Sean Regan and his shore team.

In the incident with SoftBank Team Japan, the Brits' AC50 lost its grip on the water in a high-speed turn and slid into the Japanese who were forced to fend off, and it was very fortunate that there were no serious injuries.

A steering wheel was broken aboard SoftBank Team Japan.

The damage to both was substantial but not enough to prevent either boat from continuing with the start and race. Dean Barker aboard SoftBank Team Japan crossed the line well after the starting signal. Ben Ainslie followed, after performing his penalty delay imposed by the umpires.

Ainslie was now in the hands of his shore crew who performed an amazing repair feat to remove 6 metres of crushed hull, leaving a hole big enough for a man to climb through. Ainslie had the foresight to steer the AC50 back to the

Land Rover BAR's shore crew had a massive repair on their hands to keep the AC50 racing. Amazingly, she was ready to race the next day. — HARRY KH

© Land Rover BAR / Harry KH

team's base, but as soon as he slowed the boat at the base, she filled with water — coming close to sinking.

Ainslie got no relief from the newly altered redress rules as he was judged to be at fault. Land Rover BAR's shore crew effected the repair of the Regatta to get the AC50 sailing again the next day.

Damage to SoftBank Team Japan was less than initially anticipated, and the Japanese team had decided that it wasn't sufficient for there to be a claim under the new redress code for a suspension of racing for a day, and the matter didn't go through a further process.

Round Robin 1, Day 2 — Burling gets into gear

Those who have followed Peter Burling's international sailing career will be aware that he often has an unspectacular opening day, seems to refocus overnight, and comes out with all guns blazing from the second day.

That was certainly the case on Day 2 of Round Robin 1 as he helmed Emirates Team New Zealand to two come-from-behind wins.

Six races were sailed in an extended programme as organisers tried to catch up for the lost first day of the Qualifiers.

The drama of Day 1 proved to be something of an anticlimax with the news that both AC50s damaged in the collision between Land Rover BAR and SoftBank Team Japan would be sailing in their Day 2 races as planned.

However, it is difficult to believe that even someone of Ben Ainslie's abilities could not have been slightly affected by the incident, and that appeared to be the case. The British initially led both their races, only to drop the ball and allow Oracle Team USA and Emirates Team New Zealand to stage come-from-behind wins, in Races 8 and 11.

Many had written off the French; in fact, everyone but the French. Groupama Team France provided a massive surprise in the opening

Emirates Team New Zealand race against Land Rover BAR in Round Robin 1, with Groupama Team France and Artemis Racing (SWE). —
RICHARD GLADWELL

race of the day by leading one of the series favourites, Artemis Racing, at the first mark and led the Swedes around the course by a narrow margin in the 10–11-kt breeze. The Swedes allegedly had their all-purpose daggerboards on and were caught when the breeze lightened a few knots before the start. The breeze was forecast to increase as the day progressed, and at the start of Race 2 it was gusting to 13 kts, but averaging 10 kts.

The British started well, getting a useful jump on Oracle Team USA. But this was a day for good boat positioning on the course and consistent sailing rather than having a speed edge or some other gimmick. Oracle Team USA's Jimmy Spithill simply sailed very well to pass the Brits by Mark 3, rounding with an 8-second lead. However, for a reason that was not apparent to those on the course, the British had a spectacular nosedive while sailing downwind, coming to a devastating and very wet halt.

(On the America's Cup course in Bermuda the odd-numbered marks 3 and 5 were at the top or windward end of the course. The even-numbered marks 2, 4 and 6 were at the bottom end or leeward end of the course. If a yacht was sailing towards Mark 3 or 5, she was sailing into the wind, and if she was sailing towards marks 2, 4 or 6 she was sailing with the wind behind her. Mark 1 denoted the end of a short offset or dog-leg from the start, around which the AC50s turned to head downwind for Mark 2. The finish was a similar offset leg which the AC50s sailed after rounding Mark 6 to finish in front of the stadiums in the America's Cup Village. The first and last legs were where the AC50s sailed at their fastest, often at speeds in excess of 40 kts or 75 km/hr.)

The third race, Race 9, was another 'grudge' match involving Emirates Team New Zealand with their former skipper Dean Barker, now sailing for Japan, pitching against his replacement Peter Burling.

Barker, the more experienced match racer, got the early advantage at Mark 1. Burling then started to try to grind Barker down. But SoftBank Team Japan had good pace, and Barker managed to split the Kiwis off to the left-hand side of the course on the first beat and, as they progressed, it was clear the right was favoured probably with both a favourable shift and pressure.

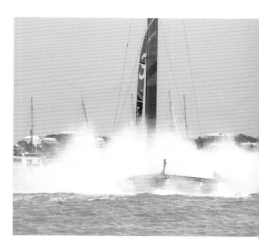

Land Rover BAR nosedives on Day 2, lifting her rudder ailerons clear of the water with the inevitable consequences (below). — RICHARD GLADWELL

Japan extended the run and led by 12 seconds. However, Burling managed to split tacks with his predecessor and surprisingly was allowed to take the previously favoured right-hand side. To the surprise of no one, it yielded the same dividend that it had on the previous leg, and Burling was able to turn a 12-second deficit into an 18-second lead at the top — a delta of 30 seconds for the leg, which increased slightly to 33 seconds at the finish.

After a vigorous pre-start in Race 10, Artemis Racing led Oracle Team USA at the first mark by a 4-second margin, which they held around the course as the wind eased to be consistently below 10 kts for the race. Mid-race, Artemis was able to extend to be 23 seconds ahead at Mark 4 and held on for a comfortable win — and handed Oracle their first defeat in the series.

The Swedish team finished the day with an unexpected loss and an unexpected win — ending the day all square.

Emirates Team New Zealand incurred a penalty for early entry into the starting box in Race 11, handing Land Rover BAR a 4-second lead at Mark 1, with the breeze flicking back up to 11 kts. However, on the run Burling eased through the British to hold a narrow 2-second lead at Mark 2, extending that to 8 seconds on the beat. The Brits managed to concede a massive 40 seconds on the run — which was extended to 88 seconds at the finish.

The British fans assumed that Ainslie was having issues with his overnight repair, a claim he denied at the later media conference, instead putting his losses on the day down to boat-handling errors and mistakes around the course.

The final race of the day, Race 12, was an interesting duel between the Defender Oracle

Emirates Team New Zealand's new helmsman came up against the team's former helmsman in Race 9 of Round Robin 1. Burling beat Barker. — RICHARD GLADWELL

Team USA and their partner SoftBank Team Japan. In some ways, it was a test of whether the Japanese team, who had been improving in recent weeks, may have gone past their development partner. Oracle built a massive 9.5-second lead at Mark 1, which was reduced to just 6 seconds at Mark 2, but Spithill was determined not to suffer another loss and eased away to win by 54 seconds.

Emirates Team New Zealand came away from the day with two wins from two races. Oracle Team USA had two wins from three races (but didn't have any races scheduled for Day 3). Artemis Racing and Groupama Team France both had a win each. Land Rover BAR came away with no wins but was held up on the points table by virtue of the 2 points they earned as America's Cup World Series Champions.

Round Robin 1, Day 3 — Emirates Team New Zealand makes the Playoffs cut

Only three races were sailed on Day 3 to conclude Round Robin 1.

The first, between Groupama Team France and Land Rover BAR (GBR), continued the redemption of Franck Cammas and his crew. A come-from-behind win gave Groupama their second win of the series and in fact the second on the trot — after their surprise win over Artemis Racing in Race 7.

The Brits led off the start and first downwind leg, lost almost all their margin on the next beat, were passed by the French on the first run, but were still well in contact at the turn. Land Rover BAR dropped a massive 52 seconds on the next beat and that was the finishing margin.

Having won just a single race in Round Robin 1 — the first they sailed on Day 1 — Ben Ainslie admitted at the post-race media conference that the British boat had an upwind speed problem. Although Ainslie firmly denied any ongoing issues from their collision with SoftBank Team Japan on the first day of the Qualifiers,

TOP: Sir Russell Coutts, CEO of Oracle Team USA and America's Cup Event Authority, explains the course to actor and Bermuda resident Michael Douglas on Day 1. MIDDLE & BOTTOM: Catamaran decks proved to be an ideal vantage point, anchored just outside the boundary at the bottom end of the course. — RICHARD GLADWELL

the British seemed to lose their mojo after the near sinking as they returned to the dock.

At this stage of the Qualifiers, it seemed that 4 points (it turned out to be just 3 points) would be the minimum to stay in the game. The Brits had 3 (one win and 2 bonus points), the French had 2 — from two wins. Artemis Racing and SoftBank Team Japan both had 2 points but didn't seem to have the inconsistency of the Brits and French. It would have been a major surprise if they did not win two or three more races of those they had available in Round Robin 2.

Oracle Team USA had 5 points and Emirates Team New Zealand had 4 — already sufficient to make the cut for the Playoffs — even if they lost their remaining races of the second round robin.

Emirates Team New Zealand and Artemis Racing had a ding-dong match, later claimed to be one of the best in America's Cup history, in Race 14, the penultimate race of the round. There were nine lead changes, as the two rival 49er helms Burling and Outteridge renewed their acquaintance in the AC50s. Both had Olympic Gold and Silver medals in the Olympic skiff. Outteridge won his Gold for Australia at the 2012 Olympics and, along with crew Iain Jensen, they had a similar run of world and international regatta success going into Weymouth in 2012 as Burling and Tuke had in the lead-up to Rio de Janeiro in 2016.

One of Australia's top sailing talents, Nathan Outteridge is very lucky to be sailing at all

LEFT: Emirates Team New Zealand performs another spectacular nosedive stunt for the benefit of the fans in the stadium during Round Robin 1. — RICHARD GLADWELL

BELOW: Artemis Racing and Emirates Team New Zealand both submarine their boats to slow down as they get close to the start line in Race 14 of Round Robin 1. — RICHARD GLADWELL

after sustaining injuries in a car crash when he was 18 years old (and the current youth World Champion in the two-handed 420 class at the time). He hit a tree while driving in a convoy between regattas, and had to be cut out of the car with spinal injuries from which he took nine months to recover before easing back into sailing, and 13 years later he was in his second America's Cup helming AC50s on the Great Sound.

Artemis Racing got the jump at the start, but was too early and was nabbed by the Liveline system — and had a two-boat-length penalty imposed. Sweden was not cleared of having taken the pre-start penalty until after she had rounded Mark 1, 54 seconds after crossing the start line. However, the chief umpire said they were satisfied that the penalty had been properly completed.

The lead swapped several times during the race with the two boats near equal at the end of Leg 6. Emirates Team New Zealand was travelling at 32 kts at the time of the mark-rounding incident on starboard tack, and Artemis Racing sailing faster at 40 kts.

At 30 kts of boat speed the AC50s are travelling at a boat length every 2 seconds, and maybe as fast as a boat length a second given the closing speed of the two competitors.

Artemis Racing crosses ahead of Emirates Team New Zealand at Mark 5 in Race 14 of Round Robin 1. The race had a controversial penalty at the next mark. — RICHARD GLADWELL

It was not really clear what information the umpiring team considered after the incident, but it seemed to be related to the potential position of the boats involved. The chief umpire said that the Liveline system did not do that, and they had to rely on the human umpires on the water to make that assessment.

Despite having a penalty signalled, Artemis Racing did not pull off the course to let the Kiwis through until towards the end of the 2-minute final leg to the finish. From our perspective at the finish line sighting up the leg, it appeared that Emirates Team New Zealand was staying deliberately astern of the Swedish yacht to protect the penalty for as long as possible — and not allowing any scope for another leader change.

Later, Chief Umpire Richard Slater said that Emirates Team New Zealand had been ahead of the Swedes at the previous 'cross' or intersection of the two boats, and the margin at Mark 6 was just 2 seconds or one boat length.

Emirates Team New Zealand had twice appealed to the umpires before rounding Mark 6. The appeals were 6 seconds apart before the umpires ruled in their favour on the second call for a breach of Racing Rule 10, which requires a boat of port tack (Artemis) to keep clear of one on a starboard tack (Emirates Team New Zealand).

As it was, the two boats finished within a second of each other, and the Swedes, although the first to cross the finish line, still had their blue penalty light flashing. New Zealand received the race win and vital point — sufficient for them to probably make the cut for the Playoffs.

'We are still shocked by what happened,' Nathan Outteridge told the post-race media conference.

'As soon as I saw the [protest] light, I knew what had happened and we were already at the line by the time the decision was made. We all thought we gave them enough room and I still stand by that opinion.

'However, the umpires obviously didn't agree. That's racing, sometimes you get the decisions and sometimes you don't.'

Two hours later, the chief umpire admitted they didn't agree. However, under the racing rules, the result of the race had to stand.

In the final race of the day and the round, SoftBank Team Japan led around every mark, finishing a massive two and a half minutes ahead of Groupama Team France as the breeze increased to over 17 kts. The Dean Barker-skippered Japanese entry was proving to be impressive, as would be expected given their leg-up from Oracle Team USA. Their speed looked good, and they always seemed to be ready to pounce and capitalise on any error by their competitor.

Oracle Team USA didn't race on Day 3, having sailed her last race in the rescheduled series on Day 2. The Defender was still the form boat of the series, despite skipper Jimmy Spithill's numerous protestations at the post-race media briefings that they were making too many mistakes for his and his crew's liking.

Oracle Team USA's newly installed hybrid grinding system (a cycle grinding position installed behind the helmsman) seemed to be working well for them. Whether it gave them as much power as Emirates Team New Zealand's four-cyclist system remained to be seen. But Oracle Team USA's splashdowns seemed to have reduced since its installation — an indication that they may have gained a bit more control as a result.

Chapter 11

Qualifier Series — the Kiwis build self-belief

Round Robin 2, Day 4

The 35th America's Cup Regatta entered its second phase with the first races in Round Robin 2 of the Qualification Round sailed the day following Round Robin 1.

There was no break in the tight schedule. In less than three days' time, the first team would be eliminated from the regatta.

The breeze for Day 4 of Round Robin 2 was expected to flick between 10 and 16 kts over the 90-minute period of racing, but on the day was a little less than that — not getting above 13 kts.

Oracle Team USA heads for the finish line against the backdrop of spars on the square-rigged *Maltese Falcon*, other superyachts and cruise ships. — RICHARD GLADWELL

The direction of the wind from the north-west meant that the course was in a new orientation from that used for the first three days of the regatta. The main difference being that the boats only sailed half the final downwind run before turning and heading for the finish line off the America's Cup Village.

The first race between Emirates Team New Zealand and Artemis Racing was a rerun of their encounter on Day 3.

The first incident arose at the leeward mark, Mark 2, where the Kiwis appealed twice to the umpires, getting a green flag (no penalty) response from them.

After avoiding the Swedish crew, Emirates Team New Zealand had their rudders break free of the water, resulting in an instant loss of about 600–700 kg of downward force from the foils and the Kiwis immediately went into

Emirates Team New Zealand chases Artemis Racing in Round Robin 2 as they head to Mark 1, often hitting speeds of 40 kts on the fastest leg of the course. — RICHARD GLADWELL

a spectacular nosedive, dropping 20 seconds on Artemis.

Burling sailed very hard and aggressively to reel in the Swedes — managing to trap them into a penalty just before Mark 5. The penalty was signalled on Artemis as they rounded the mark. The Swedish team decided not to take the penalty and just sailed out the rest of the final leg without really foiling — finishing 90 seconds back. After the race, they explained that they were conserving their energy for the third race of the day against Land Rover BAR. All in vain as it turned out.

The second race of the day between Oracle Team USA and Groupama Team France was predicated by the usual question as to which version of the French team would show up. It was the flaky Groupama Team France that appeared, with the French being uncompetitive once more.

Oracle Team USA had a wingsail issue, which proved to be more an inconvenience than a show-stopper. They were able to effect a work-around and keep racing. France finished almost 2 minutes in arrears.

Artemis Racing made their second appearance for the day — against Land Rover BAR. Most would have picked the Swedish team to have taken a reasonably easy win after the Brits' four straight losses, and after their skipper Ben Ainslie confessed to having upwind speed problems in response to a question in the media conference the previous day.

Ainslie, as expected, won the start and then confounded the pundits to lead for the

rest of the race with the Swedish team taking their second loss for the day by a margin of 30 seconds.

There was no apparent reason as to why the Brits had won. If nothing else the outcome confirmed that the boats are a lot closer in performance than many fans would believe, and in the case of Oracle Team USA and Emirates Team New Zealand the results are achieved by smart, hard and consistent sailing.

Taking an overall view of the day, Artemis Racing still seemed to be keen to push the limits in an intersection situation with another boat. While they caused the Kiwis grief in the first instance, it cost Artemis the race in another.

The Swedes were not lucky. In close-call situations, the decision invariably seemed to go against them, which must have been hugely frustrating. They were now sitting on just 2 points and should have been on 4 points, and

Emirates Team New Zealand CEO Grant Dalton sits with the support and sailing crew as they wait for wind on what was supposed to be Day 3 of the Semi-Finals. — RICHARD GLADWELL

thinking about their strategy for the Semi-Finals.

SoftBank Team Japan was the only team not to race on Day 4 and spent the day tweaking in the shed, rather than testing on the water.

Taking the Defender Oracle Team USA out of the Playoffs equation, Emirates Team New Zealand was the top challenger after the first day of Round Robin 2. The young Kiwis were looking sharper and more confident with every outing. Clearly, the hard racing practice was lifting their game on a daily basis, and the team continued to build its self-belief. They seemed to be responding well to coaching with little error repetition. If this form and rate of progress continued, it was apparent that they would be a formidable opponent indeed come the America's Cup Match.

But the immediate objective for Emirates Team New Zealand was to maintain their win rate and to reverse the first-round loss to Oracle Team USA — for psychological reasons as much as the win point.

Land Rover BAR carried forward 2 bonus points as overall winners after two years of racing in the America's Cup World Series. With that leg-up taking them to 4 points, the erratic British team had also qualified for the Playoffs.

The key focus for the Brits was to continue to win races and put their poor form to date behind

them. Their rare flashes of brilliance needed to become consistent if they were to go beyond the Semi-Finals. As the most decorated sailor in yachting history, Ben Ainslie came to Bermuda with a fearsome reputation, coupled with the impact he had made when moving up to the 'A-Team' with Oracle Team USA mid-series in San Francisco. But the boat wasn't up to the man.

At the bottom of the table, three teams were on 2 points.

Artemis Racing had sailed seven races and had three left from which they had to get two wins. Crunch day for the Swedes was set for Friday, the penultimate day of the round, when they had two races — against USA and SoftBank Team Japan.

Due to a quirk of race scheduling, SoftBank Team Japan had sailed only five races and had five left in the regatta, of which Barker needed to win two — which looked very achievable.

Land Rover BAR in their match against Artemis Racing on Race 3. Because the crew are arm-grinding they tend to stand up higher in the cockpit, adding to drag. — RICHARD GLADWELL

Round Robin 2, Day 5

Light winds gave America's Cup fans a new insight into the capabilities of the challengers and the Defender, as racing continued on Day 5 in winds that were barely above the minimum threshold for racing — a first for the regatta.

All starts had the countdown clock restarted at least once as the average wind strength dropped below the minimum 30-second average of 6 kts in the 5-minute period measured between the eighth and third minutes in the countdown.

Emirates Team New Zealand was impressive in their race with Land Rover BAR, with the British team eventually retiring to effect repairs on a new daggerboard, before their second race of the day against Groupama Team France.

Sir Ben Ainslie, five-time Olympic medallist and many times world champion, said at the post-racing media conference that it was the first time he'd conceded a race in his illustrious sailing career.

Rita, the Brits' AC50, named after Ainslie's Olympic Finn singlehander, showed little improvement over her competitor in the final race of the day. Groupama Team France led around Mark 4, but couldn't match the British upwind heading to Mark 5, as the wind increased to a whole 7.6 kts average gusting to 8.7 kts on the final beat.

About 7 kts of breeze is reckoned to be sufficient for the AC50s to have the ability to generate sufficient apparent windspeed to make an efficient course downwind. In a lesser

SoftBank Team Japan's crew pack a lot lower — presenting a better profile and reducing aero-drag. — RICHARD GLADWELL

strength of wind they are, in the words of top sailor and Race Director Iain Murray, 'like a blunt saw', and just reach back and forth across the course in an apparent windspeed hunt. To put the competitors out of their downwind misery, there is a 10-minute time limit for a downwind leg — which mercifully was invoked only once in the regatta.

Day 5 was the first time Emirates Team New Zealand had been tested in light airs against other AC50s, and they responded very well to the questions asked.

The Kiwis had an average breeze of less than 7 kts for their race against Land Rover BAR, and for those with an eye to form in the America's Cup Match went around the track in 18 minutes 50 seconds compared to the 18 minutes taken by Oracle Team USA — but both courses were shortened after the start and distances were not the same — so the comparison was interesting but irrelevant. At one point the Kiwis were doing a staggering 26 kts in just over 6 kts of air — close to 4.5 times the windspeed.

Oracle Team USA looked very good, albeit sailing in 7 kts-plus of breeze. They were led around the course by SoftBank Team Japan for more than half the race after the Defender suffered a pre-start penalty from the umpires. SoftBank skipper Dean Barker sailed well — really only losing it on the final beat when they went hard left and got out of phase with the shifts, allowing Oracle Team USA's Jimmy Spithill to pounce.

When questioned in the post-race media conference as to whether there were team orders in play, Barker looked a little miffed and denied that he had let Spithill through, putting the lead change down to his decision to go left and into the wall of anchored superyachts, letting Spithill go to the generally favoured right-hand side clear of any spectator craft. It looked that way on the water too, but it was a little odd that Barker with a handy lead had elected to go left.

Rarely on this course and wind direction did it pay to pass through the leeward gate mark and immediately head to the left-hand side of the course on starboard tack. The strength always seemed to be down, and if your opponent went right, there seemed to be more pressure and a handy shift, plus starboard tack had right of way coming back, just as a bonus.

At this juncture the Challenger Selection Series was starting to fall into place.

Land Rover BAR had sufficient points from their win on this day, their other two wins in the regatta and their 2 bonus points from the America's Cup World Series to join Emirates Team New Zealand in the Playoffs.

But unless their performance improved dramatically, it seemed that the erratic British would be exiting after the Semi-Finals — where they had to survive on race wins alone without using the crutch of bonus points carried over from the America's Cup World Series.

At this stage of the Qualifier the other two semi-finalists were almost certainly Artemis Racing and SoftBank Team Japan. The question was who would face who in the Semi-Final — with Emirates Team New Zealand, as top challenger, having their choice of opponent.

Emirates Team New Zealand has lowered her windward daggerboard and the crew is crossing the boat ahead of a gybe. Glenn Ashby and a cyclor are the first across. — RICHARD GLADWELL

For Oracle Team USA, the major question was whether they could manage to gain a point out of this series to take into the America's Cup Match. To miss collecting that point, they had to lose to both Artemis Racing and Emirates Team New Zealand. Artemis Racing was scheduled to have their crack at the America's Cup holders on Friday and Emirates Team New Zealand on Saturday.

Saturday also marked the last race day before the start of the 35th Match for Oracle Team USA. Not being a challenger, they were required to sit out the Semi-Finals and Finals of the Challenger Selection Series ahead of the America's Cup Match starting on 17 June.

Emirates Team New Zealand foils fast in flat water towards the finish line during Round Robin 2. — RICHARD GLADWELL

Round Robin 2 — Day 6

Bermuda turned on champagne sailing conditions for the America's Cup crews. Bright sun, lovely whitecapped water, and a breeze in the 14–18-kt range greeted the teams who were expected to go close to the theoretical maximum speed for the AC50s. But only one skipper would respond with their top speed when asked at the media conference. None came close to the magical 50-kt mark.

On the water, the AC50s flew with plenty of very fine high-speed spray, almost a mist, in the rooster trail left by the flying catamarans.

Emirates Team New Zealand had a great result from Day 6 of the America's Cup Qualifiers. The Kiwis won two races in fine style and went to the top of the points table.

The America's Cup champion Oracle Team USA did not fare so well, breaking a rudder while training, and had to hurriedly return to the team's base in the Royal Naval Dockyard, fit a replacement and then go back out and race.

Whether the failure was structural, or a turtle strike, is not known. The sand-coloured reptiles are relatively common on the race course and pre-start area in particular — ranging in size from small to substantial. They come up to breathe, stay on the surface for a few minutes and then dive. Turtles and AC50s are not a good mix.

To add to Oracle's woes, they were beaten by Artemis Racing in the second race of the day (Race 9 of Round Robin 2) and now had two losses in the series. The team that was turning heads, Emirates Team New Zealand, had only lost one race — their first encounter with the America's Cup champion. And in that race, the Kiwis led, before being passed at the top of the final beat.

Emirates Team New Zealand set a new mark in sailing history — being the first yacht to sail a race without getting wet. In the 35th America's Cup this feat was termed sailing a 'dry' course, meaning the AC50 had sailed the course without a single splashdown. When asked the significance of this achievement, Kiwi helmsman Peter Burling said he was surprised that it hadn't been achieved before and that he expected everyone would be doing it before long. What he didn't know was that they had achieved the feat in their first race of the day and a minor computer glitch hadn't credited them with their first 'kill'. Few achieved the feat.

Day 6 was a lucky day for the unlucky Artemis Racing.

Skipper Nathan Outteridge took to Oracle Team USA's Jimmy Spithill in the pre-start and left the two-time America's Cup champion struggling in his wake. Artemis was sailing impressively in the testing conditions, and most now expected the Challenger Final to be between Emirates Team New Zealand and Artemis Racing.

Artemis Racing's win was significant in that it was over the Defender, but it also altered the points table regarding the possibility of Oracle Team USA taking the contentious bonus point in the America's Cup Match.

Fans catch the racing from aboard revolutionary *Odyssey of Hope* (top), the British supermaxi *PWC Leopard* (middle) and . . . the water. — RICHARD GLADWELL AND SCOTT STALLARD

Oracle was now on equal points with Emirates, before the final day of racing in the round-robin phase and Qualifiers. It was a must-win situation for Oracle Team USA if they were to secure the point. Given they had won the 2013 America's Cup by a single point advantage, the bonus point had a significance outweighing its actual value.

After racing was over for the day, Oracle Team USA went back out on the Great Sound for more practice and testing and were still hard at it in the early evening.

While the sailing media in Bermuda searched for reasons for good and poor performance between the various teams, maybe the name tags on the top table at the media conference gave a pointer. Peter Burling was the only one with just the simple title of helmsman — the

Groupama Team France showed early in the round robins that they lacked the foiling control of the other teams and exited the regatta on the penultimate day of Round Robin 2. — RICHARD GLADWELL

others wore two hats (helmsman and skipper), and some three (helmsman, skipper and CEO).

Day 6 ended badly for Groupama Team France who exited the America's Cup at the round-robin phase, and with a day in hand. Skipper and top round-the-world sailor Franck Cammas was philosophical at the media conference about being the first to be eliminated. One couldn't help but feel that he was more comfortable doing long high-speed runs through the Southern Ocean than the 18-minute sprints around the enclosed waters of the Great Sound.

The French exit was touted widely at the start of the regatta. However, two good race wins, over Land Rover BAR and the fancied Artemis Racing, gave the team a lot of confidence and earned some respect of Cup fans. But on a bad day, they were dreadful.

Sadly for the French, they ran out of time, their only comfort being that in a few days they would be joined by two others at the end of the Semi-Finals.

Round Robin 2, Day 7

Kiwi fans revisited the Dark Place on the final day of the America's Cup Qualifier Series.

They had been there before in San Francisco in late September 2013. It was a wound that was reopened with surgical precision by Oracle Team USA's skipper.

Jimmy Spithill did to Peter Burling what he had done to his predecessor, and now development partner, Dean Barker almost four years before.

The New Zealanders' day got off to a bad start in the starting box after the breeze dropped markedly as the start time approached. Spithill got control of the start from leeward and then proceeded to clean out the Kiwis, getting underneath them and putting them into a position where they had to keep clear.

In the end, Emirates Team New Zealand was jammed in the windward corner of the box and appeared to have started early. However, the official call was that they had not kept clear of Oracle Team USA.

Oracle Team USA took off for the first mark, with a well-judged time on distance start, showing none of the software issues that were to bug them later in the month, hitting the line at full pace taking off on the short (40–80-second duration) leg to Mark 1, with a very handy lead. The Kiwis meanwhile sat to windward and could only wave Spithill goodbye.

In the past, and against other competitors, the Kiwis had been able to grind down their opposition with some fine sailing, good speed and sound placement on the course. Emirates set off in pursuit down the first run, and while they didn't make gains they didn't lose anything either, rounding where they started about 100 metres in arrears.

Around the bottom mark, the Kiwis did a neat gybe and rounding, again not losing any advantage and looked to go up the right-hand side of the course which had often yielded a good dividend in much of the racing that we'd seen so far.

When there had been passing upwind in the previous races from this wind direction, it had usually been the boat on the right-hand side of the course that had made the gain.

Oracle crossed to cover, and the Kiwis with better tacking and some help from the right, cut 20 metres out of Oracle's lead, and looked set to nibble away at it for the rest of the beat, and then give the *coup de grâce* at the top when they came in with starboard rights.

Burling crossed in front of Spithill about 600 metres short of the top mark but then lost it again with a port tack approach and a slow tack on top of Spithill who quickly stretched out the margin to 100 metres.

After rounding the bottom mark for the last time, Spithill elected not to cover most of the way up the beat and let the Kiwis sail their own race. Here the Kiwis' tacking did not look crisp with the bottom-end boat speed dropping more than expected in the tacks and Burling paid the price each tack.

(Bottom boat speed in a tack or gybe is the speed to which the boat slows in the manoeuvre — crews try to keep the speed as fast as possible. If the speed drops too low the boat splashes down and slows significantly.)

Around 600 metres short of the windward mark the New Zealanders had another unforced error, sailing outside the right-hand boundary line and copping a penalty. They picked up a second penalty after they got a wind shift which meant they had not dropped back the requisite two boat lengths quickly enough. That made it three penalties for the day which would no doubt be a conversation topic during the debrief at the Kiwis' digs later in the evening.

The margin between the two went from 15 seconds at Mark 4 increasing to 30 seconds at the next. Oracle Team USA was long gone and picked up the dangling bonus point for the America's Cup Match.

The Kiwis had died by their own hand. They seemed to have a slight speed advantage and were probably the better tacking. Emirates looked to have their AP foils fitted — maybe the wrong foils for the lightening breeze — a factor that has been the cause of many a surprise downfall by the top boats in their series. However, foils don't make boundary line calls.

Oracle Team USA won the Qualifier round and exits the regatta as Land Rover BAR crosses the finish line in the last race of Round Robin 2.

— RICHARD GLADWELL

In the second of three media conferences, Jimmy Spithill was critical of the way Emirates Team New Zealand had sailed their boat and their crew organisation. From what Oracle Team USA had heard from the off-the-boat audio he thought the Kiwis suffered from not having a regular tactician, as Oracle Team USA does in Tom Slingsby. No one knew quite why Spithill took it on himself to dispense coaching advice, but more likely he was feeding the Kiwi media an angle which was duly swallowed and later regurgitated. Jimmy was being Jimmy.

Over the next two weeks, Spithill said Oracle intended to make plenty of changes to the boat and that a team of a dozen boat builders had flown in from the Core Builders Composites facility in Warkworth near Auckland and were already working 24/7 shifts on the America's Cup Defender. 'That's motivating,' he told the many New Zealand media gathered in the front couple of rows. 'That gets our guys really hungry to get out there and reward those guys on the shore.'

Quite what warranted such an intense and substantial boat-building effort also remained to be seen. Or was it yet another case of Spithill tossing story angles to the gullible Kiwi media?

Responding to a question from Radio New Zealand's Todd Niall, Spithill claimed their 'hybrid' grinding system was working really well. 'The shore guys think there is still quite a lot to be had there and every system on the boat is going to get a relook. We have to be going faster to win this America's Cup. There is still a lot of boat speed left on the table.' (The hybrid grinding system was later ditched in the five-day break in the America's Cup Match.)

Spithill had plenty to share with the media, claiming a leak from Camp Kiwi (but more likely to have come from the Brits themselves, who were outside the door waiting to follow Spithill on stage) which told him that they had picked Land Rover BAR to be the New Zealander's opponent in the Semi-Final.

Spithill said, rightfully, that he was proud of his team's performance on the water and their response to the pressure of a vital match against Emirates Team New Zealand. Oracle had sailed well and deserved to be at the top of the points table. What would happen over the coming week or so of Semis and Finals racing was quite remarkable.

At the challengers' media conference following Jimmy Spithill's exit, Peter Burling announced that they had indeed chosen Land Rover BAR as their opponent in the Semi-Finals. His other option was Dean Barker, Emirates Team New Zealand's skipper for 2003, 2007 and 2013, and backup helmsman in 2000.

While Land Rover BAR and their skipper had been erratic over the series, in a way, they were probably the better option for the Kiwis. Ainslie and Spithill were the most aggressive starters in Bermuda. Ainslie is a former world match-racing champion to add to his Olympic laurels. A tickle-up from Ainslie in the pre-start of the Semi-Finals could be just what the Kiwis needed.

Burling explained away the choice of Ainslie as being their best option to get through to the Finals. But maybe they would need to keep the fenders handy, given the Brit's reputation for boarding his opponent when the pre-start combat got a little too close.

Emirates Team New Zealand's cyclors keep a low drag profile (top). Skipper Glenn Ashby sits even lower (bottom). — RICHARD GLADWELL

Chapter 12

Playoffs (Semi-Finals) — crunch time

All ready — but no wind

All racing was abandoned on the first day of the Semi-Finals of the Louis Vuitton America's Cup Regatta. The four remaining teams in the regatta headed out on Bermuda's Great Sound without a great deal of expectation on the prospect of racing. For the spectator fleet, sunbathing and swimming in the turquoise waters provided a welcome diversion as they waited for the race clock to count down.

A minimum of 6 kts was required for racing, and while the breeze did eventually come in at the level required, it proved to be only a passing

Emirates Team New Zealand presents an interesting contrast in styles against the yacht Shemara (Sir Keith Mills) built in 1929 and beautifully restored. — RICHARD GLADWELL

visit. Race Director Iain Murray pulled the pin on racing at 3.57 pm with the breeze sitting at 5 kts average. Emirates Team New Zealand looked keen to race, getting up on her foils and almost effecting a foiling gybe in the light breeze. The others, Land Rover BAR, Artemis Racing and SoftBank Team Japan, showed less interest, mooching around in displacement mode but occasionally getting up on foils.

Racing was transferred to Monday, 5 June on a scheduled reserve day. The forecast was better with a good breeze promised, before strong winds hit midweek which was expected to cause further delay.

The Semi-Finals were set to continue until one boat won five races. In any event, they were scheduled to finish on the Thursday, with the following day as a spare ahead of the Challenger Final.

Semi-Finals, Day 1 — Brits have problems

Racing got under way on what was effectively now Day 1 of the Semi-Finals of the 35th America's Cup in sailing conditions — a fresh breeze and bright skies — as forecast.

In the opening race of the day, Land Rover BAR's misfortunes continued, with a wingsail camber-arm breakage just after the start of Leg 3, the first upwind leg. Ainslie was only 6 seconds behind Burling and Emirates Team New Zealand at the mark, having dropped just 1 second since

Emirates Team New Zealand picked Land Rover BAR as their opponent for the Semi-Finals, believing that the Brits were the easiest route to the Final. — RICHARD GLADWELL

the start. The Brits were doing well, but upwind sailing was not their strong suit.

Land Rover BAR was black-flagged by the umpires after a series of penalties were imposed, for sailing beyond the virtual course boundaries — the Brits had little choice but to effect wingsail repairs ahead of their next race. They were finally disqualified and put out of their misery — handing the first win of the Semi-Finals to the Kiwis.

After fiddling in vain, Land Rover BAR hoofed it back to their base looking to fit their spare wingsail. It was easier said than done with the Brits losing 20–30 minutes negotiating the Royal Dockyard entrance and manoeuvring the AC50 back to the dock and under the crane.

Time was against Ainslie's shore team. Emirates Team New Zealand started the second race of the day (Race 3), while the hapless

Brits were still in their Royal Naval Dockyard base. The Kiwis went through a pre-start and crossed the start line. The umpires stepped in, penalised GBR for not starting and awarded Emirates Team New Zealand their second win from a race that lasted less than a minute.

Although the day's racing was held in excellent conditions for sailing, the only downside was that there was not more of it. Emirates Team New Zealand once again missed some vital hard racing practice that Land Rover BAR showed they could offer.

The first race had been shaping up to be a cracker. Burling was well in control of the start and was set to ease away upwind, but not after a high-flying hull experience as he rounded Mark 3, reminiscent of the team's near-capsize in the 2013 America's Cup. However, the 49er Olympic Gold medallist soon had the situation under control, and Emirates Team New Zealand was sailing impressively in the south-west breeze puffing to 17 kts.

The other pairing of the Semi-Final was a more even affair with Artemis Racing and SoftBank Team Japan scoring a win each. Both races saw a lead change halfway through the race, with Artemis Racing being the leader for the start and first couple of legs. But they were caught and passed when SoftBank Team Japan opted for the right-hand side of the beat, which once again paid its usual dividend.

Artemis Racing races against SoftBank Team Japan in the other Semi-Final on the fast leg from the start to Mark 1 which could take as little as 45 seconds. — RICHARD GLADWELL

Dean Barker then went to the left-hand boundary and crossed ahead of Artemis Racing to establish a handy 21-second lead at Mark 3. He controlled the race well to maintain a comfortable 17-second lead downwind to the next Mark 4 and then eased away to lead by 27 seconds at the end of the second beat and 22 seconds at the finish. SoftBank Team Japan retained a comfortable 17-second lead at the next mark and then eased away to lead by 27 seconds at the end of the second beat and 22 seconds at the finish.

Barker started the way he had finished in his second race of the day, after an even start with Artemis Racing. SoftBank Team Japan stretched out to a 14-second lead and looked to be sailing away. Barker tripped while crossing the boat during a gybe — reducing the Japanese challenger's lead to just three boat lengths, or 6 seconds. Fortunately he just sprawled on the trampoline net between the hulls, without going overboard.

Artemis Racing gained a narrow 5-second lead and stretched it to 22 seconds on the next downwind leg by sailing better angles than Barker, who often showed better speed. Artemis extended on the reach to the finish.

The two teams were now equal on the points table with the prospect of an extended series in the first to five wins/best of nine series.

At the media conference, Ben Ainslie elaborated on their issue with the wingsail.

'We split down the first run and came around the bottom gate close behind Emirates Team New Zealand. We did a nice rounding, and it was at the end of that rounding that we heard a crunching sound from the wing.

'In that situation, it is too easy to ignore it and keep pushing hard. We were lucky we stopped when we did, otherwise, we would still have been out there picking bits of carbon out of the bay.'

Ainslie wouldn't elaborate on exactly what broke, citing competitive reasons ('it is a very technical piece of kit'), but he confirmed that they had a catastrophic breakdown in a control system. He said they expected to be out sailing the next day with the system repaired and using the same wingsail.

When the AC72s and then the smaller AC50s were used, it was claimed that they would be able to change wingsails between races if necessary. Land Rover BAR proved that wasn't always possible. (Although with some slick work Emirates were able to do just that on a dramatic next day.)

'The issue was that we couldn't sail the boat and had to use our chase boats to push the AC50 backwards and sideways to get back to the dock — which took a good 20 to 30 minutes, which put us out of the second race.

'We'll come back stronger tomorrow,' he added.

Semi-Finals, Day 2 — pitchpole

Emirates Team New Zealand suffered a very challenging day on the Great Sound on Day 2 of Semi-Finals racing, damaging two wingsails, and pitchpoling their AC50 in conditions that were close to the upper limit for racing.

Fortunately for the Kiwis they scored a come-from-behind win in the first race of the day which put them 3–1 up in the knock-out series against Land Rover BAR.

All teams were out on the Great Sound for a

practice session before racing in the afternoon. Emirates Team New Zealand damaged the lower section of their wingsail during training and elected to return to the team base and replace it with their second wingsail. This was the shore crew pit stop that the British team was unable to achieve on the first day of the Semi-Finals, costing them the second race on Day 1.

Emirates Team New Zealand returned to the race course and was late to the start area. Fortuitously, the wind exceeded the average maximum limit for racing at least twice, resulting in two 8-minute delays while the 'rolling boxcar' system of averaging windspeed measurement was restarted.

Land Rover BAR had always looked very comfortable at the top end of the breeze, and the question of the day was whether Emirates could match the hard-driving Ainslie. By this

stage winds were hovering around 22 kts, just a couple of knots under the 24-kt maximum, and rain was beginning to settle in — the first serious rain in Bermuda for a month.

The New Zealand team elected to play it cautiously at the start and trailed the British for the first three legs as the boats hit the highest speeds yet seen in the regatta, sailing in very marginal conditions and reduced visibility as the murk descended on the racing area.

On the second windward beat, Peter Burling and crew put the hammer down and showed blinding speed and superb tacking to go from being 11 seconds behind to 9 seconds ahead of the British on the 1.2-nautical-mile leg to

Emirates Team New Zealand leads Land Rover BAR onto the windward leg of Day 2 as the winds gust to 23.5 kts. — RICHARD GLADWELL

windward. There was no lucky shift in it — just sheer boat speed. Maybe the Kiwis had their hand forced to reveal a secret they had been rumoured to have all regatta.

Burling's margin increased to the point where eventually Ainslie decided seamanship was the order of the day and backed off the hard-driving approach for the rest of the course, finishing over 2 minutes behind Burling.

The question as to whether the Kiwis could match the Brits in a big breeze had been answered.

The third race of the day got under way between Artemis Racing and SoftBank Team Japan as conditions deteriorated still further. We'd seen SoftBank Team Japan nosedive upwind and dig her windward hull in back to the crossbeam in the previous race. Now the rain, wind and murk was intensifying.

In the third race of the day, Dean Barker quickly had a comfortable margin over the Swedish team, who were once again not flavour of the day with umpires. Outteridge and his crew were being pinged with multiple penalties, which forced them to stop the boat soon after the start of the first beat to resolve the penalties.

At that point they were some 46 seconds behind SoftBank Team Japan who had all but disappeared in the racing and mist. The frustration of the situation got to Iain Percy, double Olympic Gold medallist and one of the world's truly great sailors, who let fly over the onboard audio. No swearing but just wanting to know what they had to do as he shouted above the storm. Alongside him in the photo boat we could clearly hear him. Percy was ferocious and justifiably so.

Conditions brightened somewhat for the start of the fourth race of the day between Land Rover BAR and Emirates Team New Zealand. Again, the Kiwis played it cautiously in the marginal conditions. Both competitors suffered penalties for early entry which were offset.

British skipper Ben Ainslie chased the Kiwis to the southern side of the starting box with both boats holding up until the start signal. Ainslie was the first to break and go, followed by Emirates Team New Zealand.

The Kiwis got foiling and up to speed before the bows suddenly dipped and then the AC50 went into a full pitchpole. From the photo boat the reason for the pitchpole was not clear as the boat was in level flight and appeared to be accelerating albeit at a quicker rate than Ainslie who was a few boat lengths ahead.

As we'd seen on a couple of occasions earlier in the series, it was relatively easy for the AC50s to get the bow down, lifting a rudder-aileron clear of the water even just for a moment, and releasing 700 kg of downward pressure from the back of the boat.

At best there would be a major splashdown with the boat stopping completely.

Or, as happened on this day, the boat nosedives and pitchpoles. On the photo boat we'd expected someone to pitchpole or capsize that day and had gone to the first mark in the first race as the AC50s came through at full speed and then had to pull away and go through the 'Death Zone' before heading for Mark 2 at the bottom of the course. But Barker and Outteridge both handled it well.

A photo and video analysis later revealed

Emirates Team New Zealand pitchpoles on the start line on Day 2 after accelerating too quickly in the 23-kt breeze. — RICHARD GLADWELL

Emirates had lifted their rudders clear of the water, and at that point the nosedive became inevitable. They were at close to the same speed as Land Rover BAR. However, it was the rate of acceleration that appeared to be the problem, as they went through what sailors call the 'Death Zone' when all high-performance boats are at their most vulnerable.

Three crew were dropped into the water, but the designed flotation and safety systems came into play, and the AC50 just sat bows down waiting for rescue tenders to move in.

Steering the AC50 into a rightable situation with her wingsail tip pointing into the wind, and then righting the catamaran, took about 10 minutes, and a lot of patience, as the chase crew let the wind do the work for them. Damage didn't look too bad — the top back element of the wingsail suffered some shredding damage and broken frames. The top front element suffered skin damage. There was substantial damage to the lightweight beam foiling. The full extent of the damage to wingsail and platform had to wait for a thorough assessment ashore.

After righting the AC50, it was strapped alongside the team tender and sideslipped back to the team base in the Royal Naval Dockyard

The support and sailing crew assess the damage as Emirates Team New Zealand's AC50 is lashed alongside the chase boat ready for the 40-minute passage to the base.

— a trip that took about 40 minutes in heavy rain which killed the wind, and made the end of the trip to the team base slightly easier.

Once at the base, the team put a man up on a halyard, and pulled the wingsail, before moving it all into a boatshed away from prying eyes and cameras.

Shredded crossbeam fairing was the most obvious damage, along with the wingsail. What could not be seen was damage to the hydraulics and electronics — which would probably take the longest to trace and fix. Water got into the forward section of the hulls and had to be bailed or pumped out.

After another herculean effort by the shore crew, and the whole team, Emirates were able to sail the next day, with a wingsail put together using the first wing damaged in the morning practice. Grant Dalton's later comment was that if Emirates had been required to race the next day, they would have been beaten by Land Rover BAR as Emirates would not have been able to repair the crossbeam fairings. That could have made for a nervous 3–4 scoreline going into the last day of the Semi-Finals.

Semi-Finals, Day 3 — a storm ashore

Strong winds were expected for the afternoon of the third day of the Semi-Finals, and racing was called off around midday.

Despite the low likelihood of racing, Regatta Director Iain Murray went ahead with his regular mid-morning media briefing.

He soon came out firing bullets over claims in Kiwi media that racing should not have been staged on Day 2. Comments made on Radio

Sport were picked up by NZME and looped back to Bermuda. After running through the standard presentation of expected wind conditions, pairings for the Semi-Finals, course layouts and locations and race start times, the floor was thrown open to questions from the 30 or so media gathered.

Second question in the session came from Radio New Zealand's Todd Niall, asking whether, in hindsight, it was safe to race the AC50s in the previous day's winds of just under the limit.

Murray responded with a prepared salvo of slides showing wind strengths for the start in which Emirates Team New Zealand nosedived, along with relevant points from the Protocol, and racing rules.

Murray's key message was that he could only work within the parameters set and agreed by the teams. Of particular note was a change to the Protocol made just two weeks before the start of the regatta when an amendment was made both reducing the upper wind limit of 25 kts and the way in which it was measured.

Murray's line was that for some time he had been advocating a reduction in wind strength from 25 to 24 kts, and a change to the way in which it was measured. However, his advice was only acted upon by the competitors two weeks before the start of the Challenger Selection Series. Murray was quick to point out that it was changed by the unanimous agreement of all competitors.

His final slide was of wind readings 10 seconds before Emirates Team New Zealand's pitchpole which showed winds of 21.7 kts for the period.

Murray commented: 'Unfortunately, we are in a sailing regatta. This week we have had

possibly too much wind. That is the luck of the draw.

'At the end of the day, the best sailors will win, whether it is light or heavy.'

He also noted: 'The boats are high performers. As you have read the teams have many, many smart people who have told me since the inauguration of this class that they will be able to handle sailing in these conditions. It is their responsibility to bring boats and crews to the competition who can handle the wind strengths that they have nominated.'

Murray was then asked, team views aside, what he believed the maximum wind limits should be.

'I reckon 24 knots,' was his response. 'The big change from what I recommended was that we went from a 60-second average to a 30-second average [in the measurement of wind strength using the so-called "rolling (box car)" average].'

Murray recapped the circumstances of Day 2's Semi-Finals racing, in regards to Emirates Team New Zealand and their actions and decisions.

'Emirates Team New Zealand damaged the lower section of their wingsail,' he said (before racing got under way).

'They returned to the dock doing 44 knots. They changed their wingsail from their Reserve Wing to their Race Wing, which they had been preserving for the America's Cup, to expedite their return to the race course to race two more races. It was a decision made by Team New Zealand to take their best wing to the race course.'

(Emirates Team New Zealand subsequently denied this assertion and told Sail-World that both their wingsails were 'identical in every way'.)

Murray noted that Artemis Racing also suffered some damage and elected to withdraw from Race 1 and conserve their energy to compete in Race 2. Other competitors suffered damage to fairings caused by frequent high-speed dives into the Great Sound.

Responding to a question on the shape of the courses used, Murray said that he didn't think that the width of the course was an issue, but that sailing three laps was too much for the AC50s on Day 2.

Day 2 was sailed in the most marginal conditions of the regatta, asking hard questions of the teams. — RICHARD GLADWELL

Semi-Finals, Day 4 — Kiwis through to Final

Emirates Team New Zealand kept their fans on tenterhooks for Day 4 of racing in the Semi-Finals.

After pitchpoling their AC50 at the start of their second match against British Challenger Land Rover BAR, the support crew put in a solid effort to have *Aotearoa* ready to race on the following day. They got a lucky break with the cancellation of all racing on the previous day allowing a thorough work-over, followed by a 90-minute sailing session on the morning of Day 3 of the Semi-Finals.

Those who saw the morning training session reported that Emirates Team New Zealand popped their rudders out of the water again, which would have caused palpitations on the team tender.

Given the events of two days previously, it was not surprising to see the Kiwis caught with some gremlins at the start of Semi-Final Race 5, their first race of the day against the Brits when the port-side daggerboard popped up during the start. The malfunction occurred at the back end of the starting box, Emirates Team New Zealand got away 27 seconds after the British and then started what should have been an impossible chase.

Those who could hear the onboard audio claim that as Peter Burling turned *Aotearoa* to chase the Brits he said, 'Let's go and run them down, shall we?' It was a very ambitious call given the Brits were almost three quarters of the way down the first leg.

The Kiwis chopped out that deficit by the fifth mark after pulling almost 30 seconds out of the Brits on the final beat from Mark 4 to Mark 5. Certainly, they were helped by a couple of errors from the British — but mostly it was a combination of speed and smart strategy that pulled the New Zealanders through for a 31-second win.

Emirates Team New Zealand knew they were in a fight in the second race against Ainslie. In contrast to the previous race, the British took control, got in front of Emirates Team New Zealand and made sure they stayed there.

Ainslie kept the Kiwis on a short leash as Land Rover BAR employed classic match-racing strategy to contain Peter Burling and his crew. The Kiwis broke through at Mark 4, but Ainslie dug deep and got the lead back by the next mark with a 26-second gain on the leg. That was a big turnaround from the previous match.

The British finished almost 20 seconds ahead to pick up their second win of the series in the first to five wins, or best of nine race series. Emirates had four wins and were on match point.

The question for the final race of the day was whether Ainslie could repeat the feat and stay alive until the final day with the forecast of strong winds.

Burling bolted out of the start of Race 7, starting to leeward of Ainslie in an uncontested time on distance start in the breeze of 12–13 kts. The Kiwis had a 6-second advantage at the start and once again lit the afterburner on the beat, opening the gap to 32 seconds and then just kept in control as the margin flicked between 32 and 42 seconds, finishing 45 seconds ahead of the British — eliminating them from the regatta.

The take-outs for Oracle Team USA and

Artemis Racing would be to stop Burling from being allowed to sail his own race.

Let the genie out of the bottle, and you'd never get him back. But in a tight match-race situation, the Kiwis were still very controllable.

Burling and his crew did not sail with the same bravado that had previously been a feature of their sailing. There may have been some wrinkles with the boat after the nosedive, and for the first two races at least they played it very cautiously. The crew's nerves looked a little frayed and they needed time to get their confidence back, particularly for those in the crew who were not from a sailing background.

Getting back on the horse after a fall is a trite comment — and doing this in the context of an AC50 in the Semi-Finals of a Louis Vuitton Trophy against the most accomplished sailor in the sport and a world match-racing champion

Emirates Team New Zealand leads Land Rover BAR around Mark 2 in Race 1 of the Semi-Finals, just before the British boat pulled out with a broken cross-arm on her wingsail. — RICHARD GLADWELL

to boot was a big ask. To their great credit, the young Kiwi crew rose to the personal and competitive challenge.

In the other pairing Artemis Racing dealt with SoftBank Team Japan in three races, taking the score in the other half of the Semi-Finals back to 3–3.

Sailing in winds of 14 kts, SoftBank Team Japan was penalised at the start of their first race against Sweden's Artemis Racing. Nathan Outteridge extended Artemis Racing's lead to 13 seconds on the first beat, with Dean Barker chopping that to a close 9 seconds at the end of the second beat, but then slid back to be 38 seconds astern at the finish.

The second match was more of the same but closer, with Artemis leading at the first mark by 10 seconds and then holding that gap until the final windward mark when the Swedish stretched to 17 seconds and then extended to 27 seconds at the final mark and finish line.

Their third and final race of the day was the most closely contested and certainly the best of the day, with Barker keeping the game

tight, staying ahead of the trailing Artemis by 6–12 seconds until the final beat as the wind lightened down to 11 kts.

At the windward mark for the last time, Artemis came in on port, with SoftBank Team Japan on starboard. On the final approach to the mark, Artemis was the inside boat and entitled to room at the mark, which Barker appeared to have allowed. However, Outteridge on Artemis looked to hold on for a fraction of a second more than necessary, making a point to the umpires before making a spectacular and perfectly executed crash tack to round the mark.

The umpires called it the way of Sweden, for once, given that on at least two occasions Artemis Racing had been on the sorry side of marginal or incorrect calls. For all the grief between Artemis Racing and the umpires this regatta, this was a call they had to win — and did.

SoftBank Team Japan dropped back to be 44 seconds astern at the final mark and 105 seconds at the finish as they throttled back on the final leg, when the wind shifted to the south and dropped to just over 10 kts.

Artemis Racing achieved the unlikely — going to four wins over SoftBank Team Japan, with just one race required to become the other finalist. SoftBank Team Japan needed two wins to sew up the second finalist spot.

Semi-Finals, Day 4 — Artemis wins through

Wind at close to the top end of the scale greeted Artemis Racing and SoftBank Team Japan for two scheduled races in the second Semi-Final.

Emirates Team New Zealand was already through to the Challenger Final.

The turquoise waters of the Great Sound in Bermuda were dotted with white caps as the two challengers headed out of the Royal Naval Dockyard.

SoftBank Team Japan hit a submerged object (a turtle?) when travelling at 16 kts, about 30 minutes before the start. There was insufficient time for her to haul out. However, divers were tasked with an underwater inspection which found nothing. The episode did cost Japan valuable practice time to get boat handling properly coordinated in the testing conditions, and that incident played a big part in their racing.

Artemis Racing had spent their morning in an extensive practice session off their Morgan's Point base at the top of the Great Sound. Vintage Iain Percy.

Officially, winds were averaging 19.5 kts with a peak of 21.6 kts at the start of the 5-minute wind measurement system, the breeze reduced by a knot in the crucial period before the start, and 3 minutes out from the designated start time the start was given the all clear by Race Director Iain Murray. The winds did increase during the race but did not go over the pre-start limit, and once a race had started, it couldn't be stopped for a blown wind-limit.

Dean Barker started well and led for the first two legs, but dropped 23 seconds on the first beat and, once through, Sweden never looked like being beaten.

That gave Artemis Racing four wins on the trot and, together with their win from the first day, was sufficient for the Swedes to go through to join Emirates Team New Zealand in the Challenger Final.

Chapter 13

Playoffs, Finals — a game of consequences

Finals, Day 1

Foil-spotting and hypothesising became a favourite pastime for those watching the America's Cup and reached its zenith on the opening day of the Challenger Final.

The wind according to official sources was predicted at 11–14 kts at race start time just after 2 pm, indicating that all-purpose foils had been the order of the day to shore crews. The wind was predicted to drop slightly over the two-hour racing period. On Predictwind.com lighter winds of 9 kts were forecast, dropping further as the afternoon progressed. That meant light-air foils were the best option.

Blair Tuke changes a jib ahead of Race 2 on Emirates Team New Zealand between races on Day 1 of the Challenger Final. — RICHARD GLADWELL

The key decision for both teams, Artemis Racing and Emirates Team New Zealand, was whether to opt for light-weather high-lift daggerboards to get early foiling and assist foiling through the tacks. Or, if teams were confident of foiling, they would take the narrower, lower-drag AP board giving faster speed.

With poor weather analysis, selecting the wrong daggerboards and with three races scheduled, the Final could be over almost before it started.

The morning of the start of the Challenger Final, media were advised that the Defender Oracle Team USA had invited both of their fellow signatories to the so-called 'Framework' agreement to train with them on the Defender area. As Challenger candidates, Emirates Team New Zealand and Artemis Racing could train this day on the actual area to be used for the day's racing.

For the last few Louis Vuitton Cups, the Challenger and Defender have had an alternating right of access to train on the course location for the racing in that day. Getting access to the actual race area gave teams the chance to pick up any nuances that might be there, and with a chance to tweak the boat in the three hours remaining before the race start. Otherwise, they could only get access to the course in the hour before race start time.

As widely expected, and all but confirmed at the previous evening's media conference by Dean Barker, the just eliminated SoftBank Team Japan skipper said the Japanese would take the near unprecedented move of training against the Defender. Barker explained this away as a means of returning the support given to SoftBank Team Japan by Oracle Team USA, who as Defender had elected not to exercise their right to build a second AC50. Once the partnership deal with SoftBank Team Japan was signed, there was really no need for the Defender to build a second AC50.

The subject of whether Oracle Team USA had one boat or two was a source of media fascination and speculation right through to almost the last day of the America's Cup itself. For some reason there was a theory doing the rounds that if Oracle Team USA was getting beaten by the Challenger, then its nuclear option was to stage a massive collision which destroyed both boats. But the theory was that because Oracle Team USA had the right to build a second AC50, then they either had it ready to go in the shed or could switch bows onto the Japanese boat which had also been built by

Artemis Racing, SoftBank Team Japan and Oracle Racing line up for a morning practice session before the Challenger Final. — RICHARD GLADWELL

Oracle's builder Core Builders Composite.

At Sail-World we'd known since June 2016 that there was no second AC50 for Oracle, and that decision had probably been made a year earlier than that when SoftBank Team Japan became a reality.

The reasons for no second AC50 were quite obvious after a few minutes' study of the rules. Under the Protocol the launch date and use of Oracle's second AC50 was quite limited — its main use was as a trial-horse in the two weeks after Oracle Team USA exited the Qualifier Round.

The partnership deal with the Japanese gave the Defender a lot more scope both in information sharing and two months' more on-the-water sailing time. Plus, if SoftBank Team Japan remained in the Challenger Series and came up against Emirates Team New Zealand then the Defender would have very useful benchmark information on the Kiwis who emerged from the Qualifiers as top Challenger.

Emirates Team New Zealand had sidestepped that scheme by picking Land Rover BAR for the Semi-Final, or rather not selecting SoftBank Team Japan as their opponent.

The Defender could still get a gauge on Emirates Team New Zealand's performance in the Final by getting a read on Artemis Racing from any hook-up they may have managed in the pre-race practice on the same course — and then making a deduction as to their own performance had they been competing in the Final. It wasn't a perfect exercise, but at best it gave a few pointers for the ongoing competitive analysis process.

That rather complicated situation explained the scene that morning looking out from the America's Cup Media Centre right on the edge of the Great Sound of two challengers and the Defender sailing around on the course they wouldn't be using for racing.

Emirates Team New Zealand, ever the Lone Wolf, was left to prowl alone on the afternoon's race course location area for the morning.

On the Great Sound, the venue for Day 1 of the Challenger Final where the first three races in the first to five/best of nine series would be raced, the south-west breeze, coming from the top of the Sound, was 8.5 kts, gusting to 9.5 kts — about 3–4 kts below the

All the New Zealand team lend a hand to wash and dry (top). Debriefs between races (middle). Dalton and Shoebridge (left) chat in the bow (bottom). — RICHARD GLADWELL

forecast at start time.

The word among the spotters was that Artemis Racing had opted for their light-weather foils, while Emirates Team New Zealand had gone for their all-purpose set-up, anticipating a freshening breeze later in the afternoon. But Kiwi hearts sank as it was obvious before the start that *Aotearoa* was struggling to do a foiling gybe — a sure sign that the higher-speed, lower-lift foils were fitted.

For the first race, given the Bermudian geography and reduced windspeed, Race Director Iain Murray reduced the leg length to

just 0.88 nautical miles — the first time in the regatta that the leg length had been less than 1 nautical mile. It was the correct call with the time taken for the race being on the long side at 19 minutes 20 seconds.

Surprisingly, despite having what was ostensibly the wrong set of foils fitted, Emirates Team New Zealand recovered from a less than perfect start to pass Artemis Racing as the Swedes did a slow tack underneath the Kiwis midway up the first beat.

Artemis made an unforced error soon afterwards when they crossed a course boundary after Emirates Team New Zealand had tacked away as required by the racing rules, allowing the Swedes time and room to keep clear of the virtual obstacle. Once through, the New

Emirates Team New Zealand leads Artemis Racing heading downwind on the last day of racing in the Challenger Final. — RICHARD GLADWELL

Zealanders stretched away and had a very comfortable 47-second win as Artemis appeared to give up the chase and save themselves for Race 2.

The surprise and relief aboard the New Zealand chase boat was that they had been able to achieve a win while sailing with boards that had been expected to be out of range. Emirates' set-up was more forgiving than believed, which was very encouraging for the rest of the regatta.

The breeze increased between races, with some rain, to over 12 kts, gusting just under 15 kts by the time the race started. Emirates Team New Zealand changed down their jib between races — opting for the second of three supplied one-design jibs. Their daggerboards were now in their working range.

Race Director Iain Murray stretched the course back out to the regulation 1.2 nautical miles, getting the finish time down closer to the target of 17–18 minutes.

Emirates Team New Zealand fans, knowing the board configuration, breathed a sigh of relief, but they soon had a reality check as Artemis Racing's Nathan Outteridge and Iain Percy got the Kiwis under control at the start. After winning the start, the Artemis Racing afterguard kept the Kiwis on a very short leash by getting ahead and then using classic match-racing tactics to cover the red and black boat

Emirates Team New Zealand trails Artemis Racing approaching Mark 3 of Race 2 of the Challenger Final, which Artemis went on to win. — RICHARD GLADWELL

very closely.

Surprisingly, Artemis with her light-air boards was able to hold out New Zealand with their expected advantage of all-purpose boards, the ideal configuration for the mid-range breeze. At the finish, Artemis Racing was 14 seconds ahead, taking the Final to a win apiece.

This was the chiller-moment of the America's Cup Regatta for Kiwi team fans. Their first real hour of doubt. The grim reality of this phase of the regatta is that one of the two teams would be going home in a day or two. The New Zealand fans always work on the basis that it will be the other team getting the chop. But now they could see the executioner's axe poised above Burling's crew, with the possibility looming that their team could be down 1–2 at the end of the first day.

Race 3 began with Emirates Team New Zealand having control of the start. But both boats got too close to the start line and were forced to sail parallel with the line to burn up time.

The start was close to being equal, as with Race 2 — but Artemis hauled through from windward on the short 67-second leg to enjoy a small 3-second advantage or less than an AC50 boat length at Mark 1 — and then once in front made sure they stayed there.

The breeze dropped a couple of knots, leaving the Kiwis maybe a little vulnerable with their heavier-air configuration of a smaller jib and smaller AP foils. But this was a much tighter race, with Emirates Team New Zealand showing they were able to live within just a 3-second margin of the Swedes.

After rounding Mark 3 at the end of the first beat, the Regatta Director elected to extend the leg length from 1.06 to 1.24 nautical miles — a decision which worked the Kiwis' way at the end of the final beat on Leg 5.

Iain Percy came off the pumps or grinding pedestal several times to play the role of tactician, as recommended by Oracle's Jimmy Spithill in the media conference at the end of the Qualifier phase a week earlier.

Later, Outteridge echoed his countryman's comments at the post-

Artemis Racing wait for the wind on Day 1. Emirates Team New Zealand ready for the next race day after racing was abandoned. —
RICHARD GLADWELL

race media conference, saying, 'These boats are difficult to sail and quite twitchy to sail for a helmsman. If you are trying to do tactics and driving the boat, it is a big ask and having "Perce" being able to look around and throwing in some suggestions, and some plans, makes my life incredibly easy.'

Maybe Outteridge had just put his finger on a key difference between the Lone Wolf and the other five teams — where in Burling, the Kiwis had a talent who could successfully function in tight high-stress situations where other helmsmen could not.

Maybe that explained his high heartrate — typically in the 140s but sometimes hitting 160 plus — but still looking very casual with his relaxed 'driving Miss Daisy' helming style. Ahead of him skipper and wingsail trimmer Glenn Ashby's heartrate only just made it into triple figures.

The Emirates Team New Zealand style is to let Burling have his tactical head and live and occasionally die by the 26-year-old Olympic champion's natural flair and virtuoso helming skills as he looks to exploit the smallest slip or gap.

Aboard the Kiwi boat, Burling is the helmsman and tactician, with Glenn Ashby handling wingsail and jib-trimming duties. The third member of the afterguard trio, Blair Tuke, was an occasional cyclor but was primarily responsible for daggerboard control, using what appeared to be a PLC-type control, where he could see the optimum and actual settings on a small screen and then used his control mechanisms to align actual with optimal.

A window of opportunity opened for the

The fans are very subdued at the end of the first day's racing in the Challenger Final when Emirates Team New Zealand came away with two wins. — RICHARD GLADWELL

Emirates Team New Zealand squeezes a vital 1-second win right on the finish line in Race 6 on the second day of the Challenger Final. — RICHARD GLADWELL

Kiwis at the bottom of Leg 4 of Race 3 of the Challenger Final when Artemis Racing splashed badly during a gybe. Burling's response was to do a near-perfect foiling gybe and go for the other mark and the usually favoured right-hand side. The slip-up by the Swedes was enough for the Kiwis to close to within a boat length or two and put the pressure back on Artemis as they traded tacks up Leg 5 sailing into the wind.

A couple of hundred metres short of Mark 5 in the closing stanzas of the final beat, Emirates Team New Zealand was challenging for the lead. The pressure told on Artemis Racing as helmsman Nathan Outteridge misjudged his crossing of the platform when the cata-maran straightened up unexpectedly mid-tack. Propelled by an unexpected G-force, he slipped

on the after crossbeam and went overboard, leaving Emirates Team New Zealand to sail out the remainder of the race uncontested.

'I was just looking for something to grab on to,' Outteridge explained after the race. 'There wasn't a lot there. I tried to grab some net or a part of the boat, missed everything, and ended up in the water. Once I'd resurfaced, I made a little prayer and wished the guys best of luck and hoped they'd make the cross and pull off a couple of gybes. It is hard when anyone goes overboard to get these boats around the track.'

Outteridge added that they would debrief and work out who would go where next time. 'But the main goal is to stay on the boat from now on,' he said with the flicker of a smile.

The stadium crowd, who had been cheering loudly as Artemis rounded each mark ahead of the Kiwis and roared as Artemis crossed in front of them to win Race 2, fell silent as Emirates Team New Zealand crossed the finish line to take their second race win of the day. The reality of this regatta was to be that the Bermudian fans supported two teams — Oracle Team USA and whoever was sailing against Emirates Team New Zealand.

At the media conference, Burling was sure they had passed Artemis on the beat. 'We were generating some serious power on board and could throw the boat through some good manoeuvres, and we thought we were going to have a piece of them at the top.' (Meaning they were in control, were very close and with starboard rights, and when those three factors came into play a few seconds later they would have been ahead.)

Artemis could have left their skipper swimming and allowed one of their crew to take over helming duties, and continued to race. Instead, Artemis stopped racing and sailed the remainder of the leg, with one of their grinders steering. To cap off a bad day, the Swedes were penalised once again for sailing outside a virtual boundary line and were recorded as a Did Not Finish.

'It was an incredibly tricky day for the forecasters,' Peter Burling explained at the post-race media conference. 'I don't think anyone was predicting it to be quite that light in the first one or quite that windy in the last two races. We were really happy with how our boat went across the range. We struggled a bit with the starts but had some tight-fought battles. We're learning a lot as we go,' he added. 'We were very happy to be able to fight our way back in that last race. Before Nath went off it was shaping to be a really close top mark. We only figured out why they'd slowed down when we started passing them on the run.'

Nathan Outteridge paid tribute to the Artemis Racing weather team. 'They did a really good job today, calling that it was going to be light at times. We hedged our bets with our configuration and took the light-wind option with the daggerboards. We had the right set-up for the first race — unfortunately, we didn't sail very well. We missed some positions when we should have tacked and weren't manoeuvring very well.

'The other two races surprised us — the wind built to be a little stronger than we'd hoped for, but it was impressive how our boat performed in those conditions. We were a little out of range, and I think Team New Zealand were more in range. We felt very strong against them. Had I not fallen off in that last race it would have been 2–1 [to Artemis]. It was a bit disappointing there, but we were very happy with the overall performance today,' he added, grimacing slightly as he recalled what might have been.

Finals, Day 2 — crucial day

The start of the first race of the second day of racing (Race 4) in the Challenger Final was called as even, although Artemis Racing skipper Nathan Outteridge claimed at the post-match media conference that they had won the last six starts.

Peter Burling's response was that their objective was to get to Mark 2 at the end of the first two legs in good shape and then start attacking on the wind. That is basically how all three races played out.

The problem for the Kiwis was that they were unable to break through the Swedes' cover in the first race and Outteridge and his crew slowly extended all the way around the three-lap course.

In a repeat of their upwind strategy from the first day, the Kiwis were able to soften up Artemis Racing by engaging in tacking duels on the windward legs. It was a battle of the arm-grinders versus the cyclists, a battle which Artemis was always eventually going to lose.

Artemis was having none of it and kept a loose cover only.

In Races 5 and 6 Emirates Team New Zealand looked set for easy wins after getting control in the first beat to windward on Leg 3.

Emirates Team New Zealand performs a spectacular splashdown for the spectators around the finish and in the stadiums. — RICHARD GLADWELL

Artemis Racing gave up the chase in Race 5, preferring to resolve their electrical issues for the final race.

In Race 6, Emirates Team New Zealand looked to have a comfortable lead but it misjudged a gybe angle, going around the final Mark 6, coming to a near dead-stop and letting Artemis Racing have a sniff of victory. But the Kiwis recovered to hold a fast-finishing Artemis out by just 1.3 seconds and went 4–2 in the series, which is first to win five races.

At the media conference, Peter Burling explained this away as getting the layline angle wrong.

The wind direction on this day was from the south-east, a first time for this regatta, and the course orientation was different as were

angles to the finish line from the more common directions of wind.

For the first time in the regatta, Emirates Team New Zealand seemed to have a game plan and stuck to it. Regardless of what commentators outside of Bermuda thought of the Kiwis' starts, getting time and distance right is a fine judgement call by the crew who are almost totally reliant on the accuracy of the boat's onboard computer positioning software. Starting a second late is way less expensive than a second early, which at AC50 speeds carried a two boat-length or 4-second penalty.

As the series progressed, apart from the America's Cup Match, the penalties for an early start dropped right off — having been common in the earlier round robins. The violent boat-on-boat aggression which was a feature of some teams' starting style was also gone from this phase of the regatta. Maybe this was also related to the elimination of Land Rover BAR and their occasionally tempestuous helmsman. Now the starts were fast and close.

As Peter Burling explained at the post-race media conference, Emirates' strategy was to be in contact at Mark 2, and then begin to attack on the beat, and use the speed advantage they seemed to enjoy.

It was now apparent that while the brain might be willing, the arm-grinders on the other boats were not physically able to match a sustained close-tacking duel with the cyclors. Their best shot at beating Emirates Team New Zealand was to get in front and hope they could stay there — as Artemis Racing did on the first race of the day. Occasionally this strategy would win a race, but it was becoming increasingly difficult as the Kiwis could just tack away with minimal speed loss, and keep throwing in

foiling tacks until the cover was broken.

On Day 2, for the second time in the regatta, Artemis Racing let Emirates Team New Zealand off the hook and, given slightly different circumstances, the Finals score could well have been the Kiwis on two wins and Artemis on four. But there is luck in sailing, and Peter Burling seems to be a lucky sailor. Artemis, on the other hand, had a string of 'if only' situations where the game had just not gone their way — including an umpire call that was reversed two hours after being made.

For Emirates Team New Zealand, racing on Day 2 of the Challenger Final with out-of-range boards had serious consequences for the rest of the regatta as Grant Dalton revealed for the first time after the 35th America's Cup Match was won.

'What I can tell you now, as a result of that day [Day 2], we then found some serious structural issues with the [light-weather] daggerboards.

'They had been taken so far out of range that they were letting go. We've lived with this since we've found it and they have been tested every night with ultrasound — and it [a crack] has been growing.

'Every time they have done a tack or a gybe or whenever I've said to them "just hold on, please hold on" — and they have.

'When we first launched the boat with our gull-wing daggerboards, we broke both of them in quick succession soon after launching. We didn't break them to the point where they went to the bottom. But they were both broken.

'You don't break carbon a little bit. They'd had it,' he explained.

'I remember going to get a glass of water from the meeting about 9 pm on a Sunday, and there were probably 20 guys in the room. And for that period of time on a Sunday night, not one of them looked at their phone. No one looked at their watch. We were in real trouble.

'We had to redesign the boards knowing the rules meant that we couldn't alter them. We had to scrap the boards that were there already and build a second set, and start again, and redesign them. Three things happened. First, we got the engineering right. Second, the industry around us just jumped — Southern Spars, our own organisation run by Paul Quinn and also the Jacksons leapt in, along with C-Tech and Cookson Boats who were able to make a repair. It was the entire industry going 24 hours a day for two months that turned it around.

'When I look back now at galvanising moments in the campaign, that was a big one because we were in deep trouble. We'd been in deep before, but not in that way.

'We pulled our way through that, and I think we wound up with the best daggerboards in the fleet.'

Lighter winds were forecast for the next and last day of the Finals.

Finals, Day 3 — Emirates Team New Zealand goes through to challenge

To the surprise of few and the relief of many — particularly in the Kiwi nation, Emirates Team New Zealand put away Artemis Racing in the final of the Louis Vuitton Trophy to become the Challenger for the 35th America's Cup.

The New Zealanders showed their light-weather pace with racing getting away at the second attempt in a southerly breeze of around 8 kts. This was the lightest breeze of the series and only the second light-air day of the whole Louis Vuitton regatta. The question to be answered was whether the Kiwis had retained their much-vaunted speed edge in the conditions predicted for the America's Cup Match.

The short answer was 'Yes'.

Race 7 of the Challenger Final got under way on the Great Sound on the scheduled start time of 2.12 pm and in a breeze that had been piping up to 15 kts in the build-up to the start.

For a time, it looked as if the Kiwis would be in difficulty with the wrong set of boards on yet again. However, long-time and heavily trusted Met-man Roger Badham's forecast was correct and the winds eased back to a more accommodating 8 kts as the starting gun fired.

Emirates Team New Zealand won the start and was first to Mark 1 and led at Mark 2 by 16 seconds.

On the third beat, it all started to unravel for the New Zealanders as the wind died, and they were unable to foil, suddenly looking very sticky and vulnerable. Artemis Racing saw Emirates' plight and was able to keep foiling. The big disparity in speed enabled Nathan Outteridge to close the gap on his long-time 49er competitor and training partner.

An altercation occurred as the competitors approached the windward mark, resulting in the Swedes being handed another penalty. Artemis in their royal-blue catamaran, were sailing noticeably faster than the New Zealanders and had to drop back on their line to clear the penalty.

Then the wind dropped further, and Race Director Iain Murray abandoned the race after the 10-minute time limit to complete a downwind leg had expired.

After a wait of 90 minutes, Race 7 got under way again in similar conditions to the first attempt, and right on the time limit for racing — which had to finish by 5 pm.

Emirates Team New Zealand won the start, their second of the day, and again led at Mark 1. There was no catching the Kiwis, and they extended steadily upwind and down with the winning margin being recorded at 56 seconds.

That result gave Emirates Team New Zealand their fifth win in the best of nine series, and they went forward to be the Challenger for the America's Cup. It was the fourth time in the 30-year history of New Zealand's America's Cup competition that they had been the Challenger in an America's Cup Match, the 35th edition of which was set down to start in four days' time on Saturday, 17 June on the Great Sound in Bermuda.

A proud Heather Burling holds two New Zealand flags at the presentation of the Louis Vuitton Challenger Playoffs Trophy to Emirates Team New Zealand. — RICHARD GLADWELL

Chapter 14

The long wait is over

Emirates Team New Zealand opened their America's Cup account on the Great Sound, Bermuda banking two wins from the first two races. The wins ended a 10-race losing streak for the New Zealand team in their America's Cup encounters against Oracle Team USA.

It was Wednesday, 18 September 2013, on San Francisco Bay when Emirates last scored a win against Oracle in Race 11 of the 34th America's Cup.

For all their impressive sailing in the round-robin phase of the America's Cup Qualifiers, Emirates Team New Zealand had twice been able to snatch defeat from the jaws of victory with unforced errors against the reigning America's Cup champions. From a different perspective, Oracle Team USA had experienced an even longer string of 17 defeats at the hands

of Artemis Racing, in the practice sessions and then in their two races in the Qualifiers.

Artemis Racing, in turn, had been despatched through five wins and two losses by Emirates Team New Zealand in the Challenger Final. Maybe the odds were in the Kiwis' favour and Oracle Team USA was only the third-fastest team in Bermuda.

Day 1

Conditions for Day 1 were at the light end of the scale, similar to the last race of the Challenger Final where Emirates Team New Zealand showed their transoms to the Swedish challenger, winning by almost a minute and uplifting the Louis Vuitton Challenger Playoffs Trophy.

The official forecast breeze of 10–13 kts never eventuated, and the first start was delayed due to winds dropping below 6 kts average. Generally, the breeze remained in the 7–10 kts

Emirates Team New Zealand leads around Mark 1 on the second day of the America's Cup Match. She led around every mark in the first four races sailed. — RICHARD GLADWELL

range, with bright sunlight and blue skies.

Peter Burling and his crew took up where they left off with Artemis Racing — winning both starts and more importantly being ahead at the first rounding mark.

There was a big turnaround in the start box, too. Burling didn't directly engage with Spithill in the first start, but got into the controlling position and left the Australian to do the rest. In the final seconds before the start Oracle got too close to the start line, while Emirates hung back, pointed at the start line and ready to accelerate when the time on distance readout

told it was time to launch.

At the start, Oracle displayed a serious fault which was to dog them all series. Their starting software didn't seem to be aligned with the start line position and race time and showed them as being further away from the start line than was the correct position and time. Their software would lure Spithill into the start, but too late in the final seconds, the Australian would realise there had been an error but didn't have the wriggle room to be able to escape making a premature start and getting penalised. It was very frustrating and unsettling.

Both boats crossed the line sailing at single-digit speeds. Burling took his time to accelerate before going up to 32 kts in the 7.5-kt breeze and punished the Defender, leading by 14 seconds

Emirates Team New Zealand's cyclors pack down tightly on the second day of the America's Cup Match to reduce aero-drag. — RICHARD GLADWELL

around the first mark, after taking a pedestrian 74 seconds for the leg — which should normally have taken 48–50 seconds.

At the end of Leg 2, that lead had stretched to 31 seconds or around 150 metres on the water. Upwind the New Zealanders extended out to 250 metres and packed another 15 seconds on Oracle Team USA.

Those three phases of racing answered most of the questions that were hanging over from the Qualifier Series. Emirates Team New Zealand could win the starts, they were faster downwind, and faster upwind.

Burling and his crew led around all 12 marks in the racing on Day 1. However, Emirates' performance was not without incident or error, and on two occasions Oracle Team USA looked to have the opportunity to grab what would have been a win against the run of play.

Oracle's first chance in Race 1 came at the final mark, where in a repeat of one of their Challenger Final races, the Kiwis muffed a gybe and brought the AC50 to a grinding halt, ahead of a fast-approaching Oracle Team USA. The Kiwis recovered, but their lead of over 2 minutes was cut to just 30 seconds at the finish by the fast-finishing Defender.

Skipper Glenn Ashby put the near stop down to the result of a crew error. 'Just a couple of wrong button presses. It's something that we could have done better and can work at,' he explained.

Oracle's second opportunity occurred at the end of the third beat in Race 2 when Jimmy Spithill chopped a lead of 95 seconds at Mark 4 back to just 3 seconds at the top of the beat, at Mark 5.

'We got a couple of weird helicopter puffs, and we didn't have the boat set up that well for the tacks,' Ashby explained, as he leant over the

fence for a quick chat at the Kiwi base while behind him the shore crew lifted the wingsail out of the AC50.

'I think we did well enough to keep our elbows out and kept them behind us, after a couple of great starts.

'It was one of those shifty days when a lead can be made and lost very quickly.'

Asked as to whether he felt Emirates Team New Zealand had a speed advantage over the Defender, Ashby said it was more a question of boat positioning than speed.

'If you were on the wrong side of a puff today it didn't matter if you were 10 knots faster than your opponent. To me, it was more about boat placement than speed.'

On the water, it looked like Emirates Team New Zealand was able to sail deeper angles than Oracle Team USA.

'If you could get the boat set up nicely, then you could wind it down successfully. We got a couple of good squirts downwind which certainly helped us. But you only had to go 20 metres too far before gybing and you'd lose it completely.

'It was a tricky one today — more like sailing a [foiling] Moth. You can lose a lead very quickly in those conditions.'

Oracle Team USA looked very rusty at the starts and seemed to lack match fitness after a 12-day layoff, despite having the services of SoftBank Team Japan. The Defender had been very strong in the start box during the round-robin phase of the Qualifiers — where they were one of the best performed. But on Match Day 1 it was quite a different story.

In Race 2, the Emirates Team New Zealand crew continued the form they had shown in the latter stages of the Challenger Final, winning the start by the official margin of 2 seconds, which stretched to 4 seconds at Mark 1.

Spithill reversed his starting strategy of Race 1. This time, with the boats sitting on 20 kts, he got into the controlling position astern and pushed Burling close to the start line. The difference between the two became apparent when the Kiwis were able to use their speed and foiling ability to skip out from under the Defender before flicking down to cross the start line.

The only awkward moment for both crews came in Race 1 on Leg 6 as the wind dropped and both boats sank off their foils and into displacement mode, with boat speeds dropping to 10–13 kts.

There was a second incident in Race 2 on the final beat at the top mark when Emirates came in on starboard, in a fading breeze, and elected to do a displacement (non-foiling) tack in front of Oracle. It was a very high-risk move, and Spithill wriggled hard to try to get a penalty on the New Zealanders, but couldn't quite do enough to get the umpires to see it his way.

Just after rounding Mark 5 at the top of the course, Oracle attempted a gybe in too little breeze. They got caught badly, with their bottom of gybe speed dropping to just 6.5 kts. Emirates had been able to do the same manoeuvre in the same place a few seconds earlier and sailed away at over 28 kts and an instant 300-metre lead.

After the race, Emirates' skipper Glenn Ashby was full of praise for how the rookie crew had handled the race — all of whom (Ashby excepted) were sailing in their first America's Cup race.

'They are a really good, talented bunch of guys who are coming through, and they don't have a lot of baggage from other previous events.

'It is good to be able to push them when they need it.

'The boat feels good, and they are sailing far beyond their age and experience,' Ashby added. 'Pete and the boys got us off the start line nicely, and that allowed us to get ourselves in a position where we could sail a few puffs and shifts to get that initial little break.

'I think it was much more about boat placement because it was so shifty, and it was also about technique in those conditions — how you were adjusting the jib and the wing and the foil.'

The two wins on Day 1 put Emirates Team New Zealand on 1 point — having started the Match on minus 1 point. Controversially, as Oracle Team USA won the Qualifier Series, they scored a bonus point for the Match, which meant that whoever became the Challenger would start on negative points. For the Challenger to have got the same point they had

to win two series — the Qualifier Round and the Challenger Final.

Similar conditions were expected for Races 3 and 4 after which there was a five-day break before racing was due to resume on Saturday, 24 June.

Day 2

In the opening race of the 2010 America's Cup in Valencia, Oracle Racing produced a blistering performance on the first leg when the 120-ft wingsailed trimaran started behind and then sailed faster and higher to catch and pass Alinghi. When asked to comment on this at the media conference, Alinghi tactician Brad Butterworth was momentarily lost for words and then, resigned to their fate, blurted out:

'That's Speed with a capital "S".'

The same phrase seemed appropriate to describe Emirates Team New Zealand's performance over the first two days of the 35th America's Cup Match.

Oracle Team USA skipper Jimmy Spithill echoed Butterworth's sentiments at the post-race media conference later.

'I think it is obvious that these guys are faster, and we need to make some serious changes.

'Everything is on the table,' he said, repeating the mantra so often used in the regatta by teams with boat-speed problems.

As with the first day of racing, the fresh

Emirates Team New Zealand fans crowd the dockside waiting for the race boat to arrive back at the team's base after winning their fourth race in the Match. — RICHARD GLADWELL

breezes of the Challenger Final were replaced with gentler breezes in the 9–13 kts range on Day 2 of the 35th Match. According to the brochure, these were at the high end of conditions expected for the America's Cup Match and were the same predicted by a 50-year weather analysis conducted by Emirates Team New Zealand before pitching the design features of their AC50 race boat.

So far *Aotearoa* had over-delivered on her design brief.

Leading around every mark in the first four races is more than even the most ardent Kiwi fan could have predicted. That's 24 marks — plus winning three out of four starts, with the other being called as even. What odds would you have got on that wager at the end of September 2013?

It was a reversal of both their encounters in the round-robin phase of the Qualifiers, where Oracle Team USA had wins over a New Zealand crew clearly short of hard racing practice.

Emirates got that hard workout in the Semi-Finals against Land Rover BAR, whose skipper Ben Ainslie is one of the toughest in the business, and certainly operates on the same level of aggression and style as twice-America's Cup winner Jimmy Spithill.

Established by former French skipper and America's Cup supremo Bruno Troublé after the 1980 America's Cup, the concept of the Louis Vuitton Cup was to give the challengers the same hard racing before the America's Cup Match that the Defenders enjoyed when the New York Yacht Club held the trophy for 132 years. It had done just that in 2017.

On the final day of the Challenger Final, Emirates Team New Zealand had checked out with confidence — boasting two start wins over Artemis Racing. Burling had left it very late, but he'd now contained or beaten Spithill in four starts, and that was a big turnaround from the latter races of the nightmare of September 2013.

On the second day of the Match, in Races 3 and 4, neither crews made any major errors, and the outcome was simply a straight speed and boat-positioning contest on the five-leg course.

The reduced in number but longer in length 1.38-nautical mile legs probably worked the way of Peter Burling and crew, affording

Shore crew, sailing crew and coaches relax, eat and chat after the second day of racing in the America's Cup Match. The measurer is in the aqua-coloured shirt. — RICHARD GLADWELL

them the luxury of being able to stretch out a little.

For all their hurrahs and high fives, the New Zealand fans were still feeling the intense emotional scars that Spithill and his crew had inflicted in 2013, pulling the Kiwi team down when they were just one win away from an America's Cup victory.

With a five-day break coming — to suit US TV schedules — Spithill said the time would be used to look at every aspect of the campaign to understand where the Kiwis had an advantage, and what Oracle Team USA could do to close the gap.

While there was no doubt a strong element of truth in what he said, it was equally likely that the Australian was once again taking the opportunity to play his favourite game of milking the gullible Kiwi media, getting them to speculate, and keeping the pressure on Dalton, Shoebridge and their frontline team.

Although Oracle's options were optimistically extensive, even in five days their choices were realistically limited.

One victim of their speed search was the much vaunted 'hybrid' grinding position which had been talked up by Spithill soon after it appeared. Its downside was that the high-seated tactician created even more aero-drag on a boat which was already more draggy than the New Zealanders', who looked very snug in comparison. It was an odd juxtaposition for a team who in the 2013 America's Cup had raced a boat that was very clean aerodynamically — a factor that contributed significantly to their win in 2013.

Ideally, Oracle needed five months not five days to make the very basic changes that were required.

The main points of difference were the aero-drag of the crew and how to get their bodies lower in the boat; their daggerboard design; and how to generate hydraulic power as quickly as the Kiwis.

The US team was able to address some of these issues and get significant gains offset by the trade-off of reduced boat control — which required some hard racing practice to work out the wrinkles. But part of the trade-off was losing the power from Slingsby's bike.

Much was made of Oracle getting weight out of their boat. The maximum weight reduction possible was by only 100 kg in a 2340-kg boat to get to minimum weight allowed under the Class Rule — which in turn would improve her light-air foiling performance, particularly in tacks and gybes.

It was hard to believe that Oracle, with all their skill, knowledge and resources, would have gone into the Match with a 'fat' boat that was 100 kg overweight when lighter winds were expected.

The unknown was whether Emirates had as much on their development list as Oracle apparently did. If the Kiwis had plenty of tweaks to come on their boat, as they claimed, it was likely the two teams would just be matching each other in the improvement stakes, and when racing resumed the outcome would be the same, although both would be slightly faster.

Despite having won four races, Emirates Team New Zealand was sitting only 3–0 on the points table going into the five-day break.

When racing resumed, it would not have taken too much for that lead to be wiped out with a couple of wins from Oracle Team USA — and 3–2 would be a completely different-looking scoreline from Jimmy 'Comeback' Spithill's perspective.

Day 3 — Defender wins a race

It wasn't until the second race of Day 3 that Oracle Team USA got on the scoreboard, taking their first win in six races, albeit by a skinny 11-second or three boat-length margin over Emirates Team New Zealand. It was the narrowest margin of the 35th Match for the America's Cup.

The Bermuda breeze confounded the official forecast, clocking in at over 11 kts average before the start of the first race and gusting to over 12 kts. On the water, it was a funky wind with distinct and obvious puffs and substantial increases in pressure moving down the course. The intensity of the puffs was not apparent on TV but very noticeable on the water, accounting for the marked disparity in boat speed between the yachts at times, particularly upwind.

In the first race of the day, in a 9–12-kt breeze, Oracle was over the line again at the start and was penalised, dropping back behind Emirates Team New Zealand at Mark 1, with both boats hitting close to 40 kts on the fast first leg. Next, Oracle picked up a penalty for a port and starboard infringement during a dial-down as the boats converged on a collision course on the next windward leg.

Afterwards, Oracle Team USA skipper Jimmy Spithill thought the call was unfair, and just one of a number of soft decisions which he felt had always gone the New Zealanders' way over this series.

Oracle dropped 22 seconds on the leg and then watched as the Kiwis just extended for the remainder of the race, going on to win by over 2 minutes, a margin that was flattered by two bad gybes from Oracle, where their boat speed dropped into single figures.

The race statistics seemed to indicate that Oracle Team USA had indeed picked up their basic speed in the five-day break, getting numbers that were close to Emirates Team New Zealand. But the price of Oracle's speed was control, and the splashdowns while infrequent were very expensive.

The second race, Race 6 of the series, was a complete antithesis of the first, with Jimmy Spithill winning his first of the hitherto one-sided Match.

It was a near-even start with Burling as the inside boat, allowing Spithill to haul through to windward and the vital lead at Mark 1. Emirates Team New Zealand trailed by 5 seconds around the bottom mark at the end of Leg 2.

Oracle Team USA showed their upwind prowess for the first time to lead by 12 seconds at the top mark. They came out of the top left-hand corner, which was clearly favoured with good pressure and a nice shift.

The New Zealanders were able to turn the tables on the closing stage of Leg 4, picking up a favourable shift and increase in pressure to roll over the top of the Defender. Emirates also sailed deeper to compound their gain.

Oracle looked soggy in the gybe for Mark 4, almost touching down twice, and suffered a speed drop as the Kiwis roared through to windward in a puff, hitting speeds of almost 30 kts and rounding the mark with a 6-second advantage.

The stats told the story of Leg 4, with New Zealand sailing 2874 metres to USA's 3155 metres. USA was slightly the faster of the two in average speed. The statistic was more a comment on the conditions, with the Kiwis finding a favourable shift and more pressure and riding it down the course. But that was also the story of the race, and what comes around also goes around, as Burling was about to find out on the next two legs.

On the next upwind, for the first time in the regatta, Oracle Team USA took to the New Zealanders, taking time out of them and rounding the windward mark near even in terms of margin. Oracle had a clear boat-speed advantage and quickly extended, as the Kiwis slowed to 18 kts while struggling to get around Mark 5 at the top of the course.

Despite being just two wins away from a clean sweep, Emirates allowed Oracle to sail their own race in the last half of the final beat. Burling chose not to employ the usual match-racing tactic of trying to engage Oracle in a tacking duel and using their cyclors' power advantage to wear down Oracle's grinders, as they had done with Artemis Racing, in similar situations, in the Challenger Final.

Emirates' real error was not protecting the top left-hand corner of the course, where Oracle pulled 150 metres out on her opponent on the upwind leg, and then headed back into the same corner and more pressure on the following downwind leg to set up a lead of over 200 metres, before rounding the turning mark for the finish.

Oracle Team USA leads and goes on to win their only race of the 35th Match in Race 6 on the second weekend of racing. — RICHARD GLADWELL

Oracle Team USA and Emirates Team New Zealand go head to head during the pre-start phase of a race on the second day of the 35th Match. — RICHARD GLADWELL

On the final downwind leg, Oracle Team USA punished the Kiwis, or if you listen to the New Zealanders, they punished themselves — dropping 19 seconds on the leg, and most of it at their rounding of Mark 5. The 20-second margin at Mark 6 was reduced to 11 seconds on the short haul to the finish.

This was the strongest wind day of the three days sailed in the Match to date, with the wind peaking at a whole 12.9 kts. On the previous two days, the wind strength had been mostly in single figures. It was a far cry from the strong winds that prevailed in the Qualifiers and Playoffs where only two of the 14 race days had a wind strength that was in single figures.

'We had some really good tight battles today,' said Emirates Team New Zealand skipper Glenn Ashby. 'As far as the sailing side went it was fantastic racing.

'Oracle sailed a good race in the second, and we sailed a good one in the first.

'It was a puffy and shifty breeze. We were a bit unlucky not to get the shift and slip away at the top mark for the final rounding and get the point.'

Ashby added that it was a close call at the top mark for the final time. Emirates knew that the intersection was going to be close, but felt they were going to get penalised if they tried to cross in front of Oracle.

'Unfortunately, the breeze wasn't quite with

us at the top end of the course today.

'It was a heads out of the boat type of yachting. The Sound is a puffy, tricky venue — sometimes it goes with you and sometimes against.

'It was a pleasing day all round. We got a few wobbly ones that didn't quite go our way. If you are not dialled in or are just on the wrong side of a shift, you can cough up a lot of distance,' he explained.

Questioned as to whether he thought Oracle was sailing faster, Ashby said he didn't think they were. 'It is hard to tell. I didn't think they were sailing all that well last weekend, but their boat speed was fine. Today they were sailing better. To be honest, I don't think their performance was better than Day 1 — Oracle just sailed better today.'

Peter Burling said they were very happy with their foil choice for the day. He echoed Ashby's sentiments that he felt Oracle Team USA was sailing slower the previous week than it should have been, with issues being how the crew were sailing the boat rather than its boat-speed potential.

'We made a lot of mistakes today. We can't hide that. We are really happy we battled the way we did in the first race to take a win there. It was a bit of a shame to throw away the last one halfway up the last beat. They gave us a pretty good opportunity to take the win.

'It just shows that in this breeze these boats are hard to sail really well and it is also hard to get all the decisions correct. We have definitely got plenty to tidy up overnight,' Burling added.

Although Emirates Team New Zealand had won five of the six races sailed, the official score sat at 4–1 in favour of the Challenger, because of the bonus point carried forward from the Qualifier Series win by Oracle Team USA.

Day 4 — a familiar story

Day 4 of the Match for the 35th America's Cup followed what had by now become a familiar script.

Emirates Team New Zealand won both starts, led Oracle Team USA around every mark, took 2 points, and had now won seven races.

In a regular America's Cup Match that would have been sufficient for the trophy to change hands. But Emirates Team New Zealand now had to win one more race to erase the 1-point bonus that Defender Oracle Team USA had gained for winning the Qualifier Round of the Challenger Selection Series for the Louis Vuitton Trophy.

Emirates made no contest of Races 7 and 8, sailed in a breeze that struggled to reach double figures. It was a tad lighter than the day before when Oracle Team USA scored their first win of the series.

The line from the previous day from the New Zealand camp was that the Emirates Team New Zealand crew had made errors and handed the race to the Defender. We heard that line a couple of times this regatta — and each time the Kiwis came back stronger the next day. Day 4 was to be no different.

For someone who claims to have had little or no match-racing experience prior to the regatta, Peter Burling again stitched up Jimmy Spithill in the start box. Spithill is one of the best in the business— but he seemed to have no counter to the unorthodox starting style of Peter Burling, and similarly with the other 49er Gold medallist in the regatta, Artemis Racing's Nathan Outteridge.

Whether the 49er duo had a different match-racing playbook or they were just winging it,

who knows? Having been on the water and watched both of them at the Weymouth and Rio Olympics they brought to the AC50 what they had in the 49er — an innate sense of boat positioning in high-performance, flighty boats.

Oracle Team USA did have a moment of hope when they were able to get into the New Zealanders on the final downwind leg of Race 7, chopping Emirates' lead back from 34 seconds to just 13 seconds. That's about six boat lengths and within easy striking distance — particularly if the lead boat fluffs the final gybe for the finish.

Sadly for the packed stadium, Burling and his crew did not oblige, and they went on to win Race 7 by 12 seconds.

It was a crucial win. A Kiwi loss would have proven Spithill's point that the Defender had found a new seam of speed — and were still very much in the regatta. The win for Emirates Team New Zealand pulled them over the point of no return, where mathematically it would be very difficult for them to lose the regatta — but they had been in that position before.

Race 8 put the issue beyond doubt, with Oracle Team USA getting an absolute rogering in the start box, and Spithill trailed Burling by a massive 14 seconds across the start line.

Burling came underneath Spithill 40 seconds before the start when they were well towards the back of the starting area. Burling luffed, forcing Spithill to respond or risk a penalty. But the Defender dropped most of their speed and all but stalled, as Burling bore off and accelerated for the start line at 15 kts to Oracle's initial 7 kts.

Inexplicably, Oracle Team USA sailed outside the boundary twice on the first beat, but although they were penalised, they were sufficiently far behind the Kiwis for the indiscretion to have minimal effect on the margin.

At the end of Leg 4, Oracle suffered a boat-stopping splashdown during a gybe rounding of the leeward mark. While the boat slowed markedly, the error didn't show up too badly in the race statistics, indicating that the Kiwis probably picked the wrong side of the course — a compensating error.

TOP: Shore crew work over Emirates Team New Zealand's race boat before practice on the morning of the final day of the 35th America's Cup Match. MIDDLE & BOTTOM: Team NZ takes both races. — RICHARD GLADWELL

Oracle Team USA looked to be paying the price for the removal of the BMX or 'hybrid' grinding position to lighten the boat, as they appeared to lack oil pressure at critical moments of the race. Since the removal of the bike grinding station, Oracle Team USA had suffered several splashdowns in situations where previously they had looked very strong.

Oracle Team USA rounded out a decisive day 30 seconds in arrears of Emirates Team New Zealand, going into a position where, if they lost another race, the America's Cup would be leaving the trusteeship of the Golden Gate Yacht Club.

Day 5 — America's Cup is now New Zealand's cup

The Royal New Zealand Yacht Squadron created sailing history to become the first club to regain the America's Cup, after Emirates Team New Zealand sailed to victory in Race 9.

On Day 5 two races were scheduled, but only the first was required after the New Zealand

Emirates Team New Zealand crosses the finish line to win Race 9 and win the 35th Match for the America's Cup by 8–1. — RICHARD GLADWELL

team, trailing at Mark 1, passed the Defender on the second leg and then sailed away to a series win by a margin of 54 seconds.

The outcome of the race was never in doubt, once Emirates Team New Zealand gybed first and was able to sail a faster angle to the second mark.

Oracle Team USA started with a bigger jib than the New Zealand team who looked to be rigged more for conditions in the 9–12-kt range. That was an ambitious call as it turned out, with the breeze never getting above 9 kts.

Once again Emirates Team New Zealand looked to have the better of the start, again taking up the leeward position and allowing Jimmy Spithill to take the windward slot at the start.

The US team seemed to be rigged for a fast first leg, and despite having to sail the longer distance, they shot over the top of the New Zealanders to take a 4-second lead at the first mark. Normally, that should have set the stage for a race win, which would have got the Americans back on the comeback trail, but it was not to be. Emirates Team New Zealand put 22 seconds on Oracle Team USA on the next beat and then kept a loose cover to seal the race and wrest the America's Cup from the Golden Gate Yacht Club.

Joy and relief

Ashore the fans celebrated with a mix of joy and relief. The joy was for the outstanding performance and indeed survival of the team, which had withstood attack after attack off the water since losing to Oracle Team USA in 2013 in the series that spanned three weeks and ran across 19 races.

Add to that the 1-second loss in the seventh race of the 2007 America's Cup in Valencia, the ignominy of 2003 defeat and the loss of the America's Cup on the Hauraki Gulf in the second defence.

Further back is the break-up of the then Team New Zealand following the luring of key sailors to Swiss Challenger Alinghi.

There were plenty of lurking demons in the Kiwi America's Cup kitbag, which were exorcised by the day's win.

Emirates Team New Zealand's win triggered several firsts:

Peter Burling and Blair Tuke became the first sailors in history to win an Olympic Gold medal and an America's Cup in the space of 12 months.

Emirates Team New Zealand was the most inexperienced crew to win the America's Cup — with just one America's Cup Regatta among the crew. Peter Burling became the youngest helmsman to win the America's Cup.

The Royal New Zealand Yacht Squadron became the first club to win back the America's Cup.

At the presentation of the America's Cup, there was no handover from the previous Defender to the new, as had happened in 2010 in Valencia.

Instead the America's Cup was brought to the podium by a white-gloved security guard and placed on a stand.

Peter Burling and Glenn Ashby picked up the 166-year-old Victorian ewer and raised it in triumph above their heads. The sea of Kiwi fans, festooned with New Zealand flags and wearing their team's livery, just roared. The emotion was palpable. The faces of every person in front of the stage or on it was the face of ecstatic individual joy. The America's Cup had become the people's cup.

It was a scene that was to be replicated over and over again when the America's Cup arrived back in New Zealand, and then on the street parades and receptions in Auckland, Wellington, Christchurch and Dunedin. In one of the unexpected idiosyncrasies of human nature the trophy, which Matteo de Nora said seemed to be contested between eccentric billionaires who wanted to have a go at each other, became an object of huge emotional attachment and pride for people often of very limited means who closely identified themselves with Emirates Team New Zealand and all that it had been through and meant.

At the winner's media conference, Emirates Team New Zealand CEO Grant Dalton set the agenda for a new era in the America's Cup emphasising that holding the trophy was a privilege not a right.

It seemed that there had been some discussions about the shape of the new America's Cup, but little in the way of specifics other than the year and venue for the 36th Match.

No surprise was the announcement of the next Challenger of Record, Circolo della Vela Sicilia (CVS) and its team Luna Rossa, which has a long and close association with New Zealand extending back to 2000. The Italian team are on the same page in most respects to the new Defender, and the relationship is expected to be harmonious.

The Moët comes out as Peter Burling sprays Matteo de Nora and Grant Dalton after winning the America's Cup. — RICHARD GLADWELL

The Presentation

There was no traditional handover of the America's Cup from the former Defender to the new. Instead the 166-year-old trophy was brought onto the stage in Bermuda by a security guard, deposited on a plinth, and uplifted by Peter Burling and Glenn Ashby in front of a cheering sea of fans, family and supporters. And then the serious celebrations began. — PHOTOS RICHARD GLADWELL & SCOTT STALLARD

Chapter 15

The skipper reflects

Late in 2016, when they refused to sign an agreement on how the next two America's Cups would be conducted, Emirates Team New Zealand was cast in the role of being a 'lone wolf'.

The moniker has stuck with the team since and it was the hallmark of a campaign that struggled financially, that thought differently and was forced to eke the most out of the resources that it did have. That struggle made their America's Cup win on the last Monday in June 2017 all the sweeter.

'We have been the Lone Wolf from Day 1,' said skipper Glenn Ashby. 'We have had to adopt that as our stance — as we were away from everyone. But we also had to be the Lone Wolf in our design philosophy and our projection and anticipation of where the bar

Emirates Team New Zealand skipper and sail trimmer Glenn Ashby poses in front of the AC45 foiler loaned by Luna Rossa to Emirates Team New Zealand in August 2015. — RICHARD GLADWELL

would ultimately be, in this cycle.

'We have run our own course, and it has proven to be the correct one.'

Emirates Team New Zealand stayed out of Bermuda, arriving two years after Oracle Team USA. The risk for the other teams was that they became too familiar with each other, and risked becoming clones of each other. With that strategy and situation, they were always vulnerable to a team like Emirates Team New Zealand coming at the group from out of left field, with different ideas and a different approach.

'We ultimately didn't have a choice as to when we came over,' said Ashby. 'While venue knowledge is important — like it is at the Olympics when you have to be there for years before to see what the conditions are like. But we had spent enough time in Bermuda over the last couple of years to know what sort of water we had, and to know that it was shifty.

'Ultimately, we knew we were racing ourselves. We knew where the level was

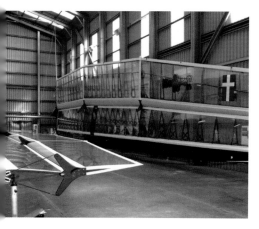

going to get to — and if we didn't reach that level, we wouldn't be competitive.

'We had to push on our own programme by ourselves.'

Ashby says they knew that they were going to have to do dry laps (full races where the foiling AC50 didn't touch the water). Good starts were also going to be essential, and the boat had to have good boat speed.

'We had to be 100 per cent focused on our own programme,' he explained. 'We knew what the others were up to, but it didn't change our path. We believed we were on the right course and didn't change our decisions.'

Emirates Team New Zealand had their preferred training ground to the east of Browns Island in Auckland's Hauraki Gulf, known as the 'Back Paddock'. Ashby says that the conditions there were a 90 per cent match with what they expected in Bermuda.

'That helped a lot with the way we set up our boat and control systems.'

Ashby says the switch to leg power for the grinders rather than the traditional arms wasn't the silver bullet behind the team's win.

'I think ultimately it was our aggressiveness in our design philosophy. That to me sums up our whole programme — we had to throw it out there. We were either going to be a laughing stock when we arrived in Bermuda, or we were going to do what we did.

'There are a lot of aspects to the programme, and the bicycles were a big part of that, but it is the full package of how aggressively we attacked the problem that we had, and we did that better than the other teams.'

Ashby said that Day 2 of the Challenger Final was the key moment in terms of winning the regatta for Emirates Team New Zealand. The Kiwis came away with two wins from three races, despite being caught out with the light-weather daggerboards in a breeze that rose and fell during the afternoon.

'My thinking was that if we could race well against Artemis in breezy conditions — given that they had beaten Oracle in 17 races

AC45 wing sails in Auckland showing the two element wingsail (top), the control arms and mechanisms (top and centre) and the aircraft wing construction with the covering film being spread and shrunk (bottom). — RICHARD GLADWELL

in a row, then we possibly might have a chance at the Cup.'

He says he knew they were going to have a big battle with Artemis Racing in the Challenger Final. 'My thinking was that if we could outsail them in these conditions, we could keep on our path and keep improving ourselves and the boat.'

On board the AC50, Ashby kept a very low profile, with one commentator claiming all you could see were his eyes peering above the cockpit edge. In his hand, Ashby was running a box which allowed him to control all the wing functions and the jib as well — which included the jib Cunningham, jib track and jib sheet. The box ran all the twist for the wing.

'Every single aero function on the boat could be run from my cockpit, and that one little control box,' he explained.

'You could do that from either side of the yacht — so we could tack or gybe without me having to get out of my seat to go to the other side.

'We could also push or pull the wing, with the sheet, which the other guys couldn't do with their standard drums. They always had to have someone holding the sheet. With our push-pull system, it could do anything we liked from either side of the yacht. That was a big advantage for us.'

The control box, in turn, triggered a series of electro-mechanical switches which controlled the valves to make the sail adjustments.

'All the buttons on the boat were set up to do the same functions — so the buttons that Pete had on the wheel, my floor buttons for getting the daggerboards up and down in the tacks and gybes, were all set up the same way.

'When you did the button press or the toggle movement, an electrical signal would be sent to the valve, and then the valve would open and allow the hydraulic pressure or fluids to go to the ram and operate that function.

'The whole boat ran off a PLC [programmable logic controllers commonly used in factory production processes] that operated the hydraulic system. It was very complicated, but well set up.'

Ashby believes that the other boats used a similar system. However, the main difference in the Emirates Team New Zealand set-up was that during different manoeuvres, the wingsail could still be trimmed from the wheel.

'I don't believe any of the other teams could do that,' Ashby added. 'They would have to reach forward while hanging onto the sheet, while we could have both hands operating the daggerboard, the jib, wing sheet and the rudder functions all in one go as well. So, we could sail the boat and do a lot of different manoeuvres and have a lot of crossover while there were people moving around the boat. It all worked very well.'

Being able to top up the hydraulic pressure more quickly than their competitors meant there could be more functionality on board the boat.

'One of the things that not many people know about this campaign was that we only ran two accumulators [a pressure storage reservoir of hydraulic fluid] on board, and not three. We decided to take the extra weight of an accumulator off the boat because we believed that our guys could top up the accumulators quite quickly, which allowed weight reduction.

'While the other boats started off with more stored energy, we believed that we could get around the track cleanly, with the weight saving, and utilise that energy elsewhere.'

Emirates Team New Zealand shows its very clean cockpit and the gull-wing foil which was broken in in Auckland and used extensively in the match. — RICHARD GLADWELL

The late Warren Jones, one of the management masterminds behind the successful *Australia II* challenge for the America's Cup, made a comment 'that to win the America's Cup, you had to make every decision the right one for three years'.

When asked whether Emirates Team New Zealand had made any wrong decisions over the past three years, Ashby replied: 'Without wanting to sound like a plonker, looking back now, I can't think of too many things we got wrong.

'There are things that we would have liked to have had earlier. But as far as the decision-making process and the decisions we did make, I can categorically state that I don't think we made any major errors along the way. You can't make mistakes at any point of the campaign —

particularly at the latter stage.

'I don't think we made too many mistakes, which ultimately made us very competitive over here.'

One of the downsides with the use of multihulls in the America's Cup is that teams seem to acquire an enormous amount of kit-boats, parts, training and test platforms. In the 35th America's Cup, some teams ran up to four AC45S test boats, plus various other two-man foiling catamarans and singlehanded foiling Moths.

Budget constraints imposed by the selection of Bermuda as a venue and the loss of government funding when the Qualifiers were taken away arbitrarily from Auckland meant that Emirates Team New Zealand scrapped plans to run a two-sailing team and two-test boat programme. Instead, they launched just a single AC45S and then the single AC50 (as allowed by the Protocol).

'We didn't have too much choice in the

matter, but by having less, we were able to focus more sharply on the future and where the boats needed to be,' Ashby said.

'For us, two-boat testing is imperative for development and going forwards. But having the vision and the people who can make the correct decisions is the key to success. I think we had the right people to enable us to make the right decisions to progress in the way that we did.'

In the 2013 America's Cup campaign, Emirates Team New Zealand built two AC72s but decommissioned the first to provide some parts for the second boat which became the Challenger in the match.

In 2013, as well as the 2017 America's Cup, Emirates Team New Zealand arrived with a boat that was quick out of the box, compared to teams that had been training for months or years in the regatta venue on Bermuda's Great Sound.

A key to this is the interface the team seems to be able to achieve between the design computer, performance simulation and then

Oracle Team USA shows a very different foil shape from Emirates Team New Zealand. The Defender crew is not as tightly packed as the New Zealand crew. — RICHARD GLADWELL

translating this very accurately to on-the-water performance.

'In this campaign, we definitely used the computer simulation side of things a lot more than in the previous campaign,' Ashby explained. 'We were forced into that by the fact that we didn't have any test boats and we didn't have any resource to be able to get on the water in those early stages.

'Dan Bernasconi has done an amazing job with this team by being able to go through the computer simulation/VPP [velocity prediction] side. As a sailing team, there was just a small core group who spent time with those designers and engineers, and together we have been able to keep moving forwards and almost predicting where we needed to be at certain points in time.

'When we launched our proper test boat it showed the rest of the world that we hadn't been sitting down in Auckland mucking around. I think we possibly surprised the other teams as to how advanced our test boat was when we launched her for the first time.'

The financial constraints caused by the loss of the Qualifiers from Auckland forced Emirates Team New Zealand to spend their early time developing computer software and design systems that would be quicker and more accurate when funding did come on stream.

'The technology, design and engineering side of things gave us, as the sailing team, great confidence in knowing that if we could keep up our end of the bargain — keep developing and keep pushing those design and engineering

guys as well — then we would have a package that was, in our minds at least, ultimately the most advanced AC50 out on the water.

'We had our ups and downs as all the teams did, but the philosophy that we had and the connectivity between the sailing, design teams and the shore teams was vital.

'That relationship was very special, and without that relationship we wouldn't have wound up with a package that is anywhere near as advanced.'

One of the features of the Emirates Team New Zealand campaign in Bermuda was how quickly the sailing crew learned and got race sharp despite losing a lot of planned time due to unsuitable weather in practice sessions and other teams refusing to sail against the 2013 Challenger.

They only really looked match-ready after the second day of racing in the Challenger Final and showed their polished act on the third and final day of that series. Five days later they

The America's Cup now resides at the Royal New Zealand Yacht Squadron, flanked by the 2017 Louis Vuitton Playoff Trophy (left) and the Louis Vuitton Cup contested 1980–2013. — CARLO BORLENGHI

started the Match for the 35th America's Cup.

'Our guys are very quick learners, and they have some fantastic guys around them — like Ray Davies, Murray Jones and Richard Meacham.

'As a group, we knew that we would lack race experience. We were hoping that we would be fast enough and knew that we would have to work hard on our starting and sailing against another boat. We'd never done that in the whole campaign. We knew we were up against it. We knew we were on the back foot. The other teams had been in Bermuda for months and some for years.

'We had practised our boat handling back in Auckland, and practised racing against the chase boat.

'A chase boat with 1200 hp of Yamaha outboards on the back is a very different sailing proposition than an AC50 in pre-starts. We knew what we could get away with in boat handling. But Land Rover BAR, Artemis and SoftBank all had very strong starting packages. They had seen it all before, and they gave us some good sailing lessons in those first few races.

'That made us stronger — and hats off to those guys for pushing us hard. We knew that if we didn't get pushed we would always be up against it in the Match.'

Ashby says the sailing team worked out where their strengths were — which was their boat handling — and also their weaknesses.

'That put us on the front foot against Jimmy, rather than the back when we finally lined up,' Ashby said.

'When you have the right guys in the right team, doing the right jobs around you, that allows you the opportunity to do some special things. You can then learn and keep learning and stay on the same path. That to me as Sailing Director and as a wing trimmer is a very proud moment, watching your crew and team create greatness. That is a wonderful feeling.'

Probably the biggest area of very noticeable improvement by Emirates Team New Zealand, as the Challenger Series progressed, was in the start box.

Ashby explained that the starting is unique in the AC50s as the boats can accelerate and decelerate very quickly on the foils. He pointed out that it is a very different process to the displacement multihull match-racing. 'There is no other type of boat in the world that could do the type of pre-starts we do on these AC50s. Some of the lessons cross over, but the decision-making process and boat handling is unique.

'All the teams were on a steep learning curve, and there was a big difference between what was happening in the beginning during training and at the regatta end during racing.

'We pushed that to another level with what we could do with our boat handling,' Ashby added.

He says that the New Zealand team knew before they went to Bermuda that they would have the edge in a tacking duel due to their extra power and ability to quickly top up the hydraulic pressure.

'We could tell that from the recon footage, as to how many tacks they could do, how often they were standing up and how many times they stopped.

'Because we knew we had more juice in the tank we could pull off slightly better manoeuvres and not be afraid to keep pushing an opponent to the point where they will start making mistakes.

'We were always happy to get into a dogfight if it had to come to that.'

Results 35th America's Cup Match

DEFENDER: Golden Gate Yacht Club represented by Oracle Team USA

CHALLENGER: Royal New Zealand Yacht Squadron represented by Emirates Team New Zealand

17 June 2017 — America's Cup Match, Day 1 Results

Race 1: Emirates Team New Zealand beat Oracle Team USA by 30.2 secs Wind at start: 7.5 kts av/10 kts gust|ETNZ led at start and all marks OTUSA OCS.

Race 2: Emirates Team New Zealand beat Oracle Team USA by 87.5 secs Wind at start: 8.6 kts av/11.2 kts gust|ETNZ led at start and all marks.

18 June 2017 — America's Cup Match, Day 2 Results

Race 3: Emirates Team New Zealand beat Oracle Team USA by 48.7 secs Wind at start: 9.9 kts av/11.9 kts gust|Start even ETNZ led at all marks.

Race 4: Emirates Team New Zealand beat Oracle Team USA by 71.4 secs Wind at start 10.5 kts av/13.0 kts gust|Start even ETNZ led at all marks.

24 June 2017 — America's Cup Match, Day 3 Results

Race 5: Emirates Team New Zealand beat Oracle Team USA by 124 secs Wind 9.8 kts av/12.4 kts gust|ETNZ led at all marks OTUSA OCS.

Race 6: Oracle Team USA beat Emirates Team New Zealand by 11.3 secs Wind at start 10.3 kts av/11.9 kts gust|ETNZ won start OTUSA led at Marks 1, 2, 3, 6 ETNZ led at Marks 4,5.

25 June 2017 — America's Cup Match, Day 4 Results

Race 7: Emirates Team New Zealand beat Oracle Team USA by 12 secs Wind at start 9.1 kts av/9.9 kts gust|ETNZ won start led at all marks.

Race 8: Emirates Team New Zealand beat Oracle Team USA by 30 secs Wind at start 9.0 kts av/10.6 kts gust|ETNZ won start and led at all marks.

26 June 2017 — America's Cup Match, Day 5 Results

Race 9: Emirates Team New Zealand beat Oracle Team USA by 54.4 secs Wind at start 9.1 kts av/9.6 kts gust|Even start. OTUSA led at Mark 1; ETNZ led at Marks 2, 3, 4, 5, 6.

Of 54 marks rounded in the 35th America's Cup Match, Emirates Team New Zealand led around 49 marks, Oracle Team USA led around 5 marks. Of the starts, ETNZ won 4; OTUSA was OCS (On Course Side) in 2; 3 starts were called as Even.

Royal New Zealand Yacht Squadron/Emirates Team New Zealand — 8 wins.

Golden Gate Yacht Club/Oracle Team USA — 1 win.

A catalogue record for this book is available from the National Library of New Zealand

ISBN 978-1-988516-09-7

A Mower Book
Published in 2017 by Upstart Press Ltd
Level 4, 15 Huron St, Takapuna 0622
Auckland, New Zealand

Text © Richard Gladwell 2017
The moral rights of the author have been asserted.
Design and format © Upstart Press Ltd 2017

Designed by www.CVDgraphics.nz
Printed by Everbest Printing Co. Ltd., China